Meadow Prospect
Revisited

Gwyn Thomas

Meadow Prospect Revisited

edited by
Michael Parnell

SEREN BOOKS

SEREN BOOKS is the book imprint of
Poetry Wales Press Ltd.
Andmar House, Tondu Road, Bridgend, Mid Glamorgan
Wales, CF31 4LJ

British Library Cataloguing in Publication Data:

Thomas, Gwyn
Meadow Prospect Revisited
I. Title
823.914 [FS]

ISBN: 1-85411-065-9

The publisher acknowledges the financial assistance of the
Welsh Arts Council

Printed in 10.5 point palatino
by The Cromwell Press, Melksham

Contents

Introduction

In his lifetime Gwyn Thomas published nine novels and four collections of short stories. In addition to the seventy-four short stories and novellas contained in his four collections, he wrote many that were not collected; of these some were read on the air in BBC radio story slots, some were published in magazines as diverse as *Coal* and *Vogue*, several appeared in Canada and the USA in such magazines as *Masses and Mainstream*, *The Reporter* and *The Montrealer*, but most were written at the behest of those perceptive editors of *Punch*, Malcolm Muggeridge and Bernard Hollowood.

In the greater part of all his fiction of no matter what length, Gwyn Thomas's chief preoccupation was with the small but intense, dark and sometimes dramatic world of his native Rhondda Valley. He was born in 1913 in Cymmer, Porth, the youngest of the twelve children of a generally unemployed and always indigent coalminer. His mother died in 1919 and the running of the family was taken over by the youngest of the four daughters, seventeen-year-old Hannah. Known as Nana, she managed wonderfully well; the young Gwyn experienced as happy a childhood as one could hope for in such circumstances, when money, food, and clothes were in barely adequate supply. Throughout his life he carried a burthen of vivid recollections of living and growing through the economic difficulties of the 20s and 30s. Himself unemployed almost continuously between 1934 and 1940, despite his Oxford degree, he looked with tender admiration on the way his people conducted themselves in those hard times. When he came to write, his subject was to hand, and a stream of stories began to pour from him recalling, celebrating, and gently mocking the characters of the world he had lived in and which now recreated itself in his mind as a universal world of great vitality.

Never a completely consistent man, he did not work out the geography of his world with anything like the fanatical attention to detail of, say, a Tolkein. Always recognisably some part of the Rhondda or its immediate environs, and named with due respect for the style of the region, his townships nevertheless are not easy to locate either on the real or on an imaginary map. The centre of the world in the earliest books is a couple of rows of terraced houses set halfway up a mountain overlooking a colliery and overhung by the black tip of spoil from the pit; the area is known simply as 'The Terraces' and the town of which the terraces are a part seems to merit no name. But Gwyn Thomas was a keen student of nomenclature and took a huge delight in names. In other stories written at about that time the road climbing to the terraces from the town is called 'Windy Way'; the town itself seems to emerge as Mynydd Coch ('Red Mountain'). Not far away the larger community of Birchtown begins to be glimpsed, and the axis between them is the axis between Porth and Pontypridd.

The apparent stability crumbles, however. The town of Ferncleft comes into the picture, apparently, like Tonyrefail in real life, on the outside of the wall of hills dividing the Rhondda from the coastal plain and the Vale of Glamorgan. Unlike Tonyrefail, however, Ferncleft is sometimes three miles from the sea and sometimes eight. At about this time the place we had thought of as Mynydd Coch turns up in the novel *The Thinker and the Thrush* as Bandy Lane, but in later stories appears to modulate its name to Meadow Prospect, perhaps because Mynydd Coch's cemetery, known as the Black Meadow, becomes symbolically more dominating, eventually diverting significance from the red mountain and imposing a new, more sardonic cognomen upon the village it serves. Alongside the Black Meadow runs the village's black, coal-dust tainted and otherwise polluted river, most commonly called the Moody, but just occasionally flourishing under other names.

In many of Gwyn Thomas's shorter fictions a town called Belmont is the scene of the action. No doubt a suitably motivated postgraduate student could usefully devote an entire thesis to discovering whether or not this is yet another name for the imaginary town Thomas created from his memories of Porth, devoting at least a chapter to the identification of all the cinemas that abound in the area. Most enduringly and memorably called Meadow Prospect, this little world remained at the heart of almost all Gwyn Thomas's story-making for over thirty years, not only in his short stories and more extended prose fictions, but also in the radio plays and later the television plays which introduced his name to a different public.

The idea of this book is to bring back into circulation a number of his reflections and divertissements on the topic of Meadow Prospect and its inhabitants which have not been available for many years; most of which have not, in fact, ever been published in book form before, and some of which have never been published at all on this side of the Atlantic. It does not, as it were, make any attempt at presenting a complete history and topography of Meadow Prospect, for that would entail reprinting material from books already published under Gwyn Thomas's name. We should like this to come as a new book full of delightful surprises not only for those too young perhaps to know of Meadow Prospect from previous reading but also for those who already treasure the information in *Where Did I Put My Pity?*, *Gazooka*, *Ring Delirium 123*, *The Lust Lobby*, and *A Welsh Eye*.

The stories in this collection were written and published at various times and in various places between 1946 and 1979. They may be divided broadly into two kinds: those which are more obviously autobiographical and terminologically accurate (in as far as Gwyn Thomas could ever be said to have written without evident recourse to fiction and its methods); and those which are clearly intended as fictions (though those in the know will recognise the actual or real-life situations and people from which the germ of the story probably derived). And in between them, as if to make such definition practically impossible, there are some pieces which are a bit of both. Not that it matters, but one tries to impose some tidiness on the situation! I have put the more straightforwardly autobiographical pieces first, and allowed the fiction-making process to take charge in the later stories. These have been grouped according to location, period and character-list; some readers may feel that this gives them a coherence not greatly inferior to that achieved by Gwyn Thomas in some of the books he called novels. Full details of original publication are provided (where they are known) in a brief postscript for those who like to know these things.

The editor can only hope that readers may derive as much pleasure from their perusal of the book as its preparation has afforded him. And those who have really enjoyed it may be glad to be assured that there are other Gwyn Thomas books, some old, some quite new like this one, in the pipeline. A few thousand children were invited in an examination recently to read a passage from Gwyn Thomas's autobiography, *A Few Selected Exits,* and make some comments on it. Although it was plain that few of them had ever encountered his writing before or even knew his name, they almost without exception declared their delight in what they had read and their intention to find more of this stuff of comic genius to feast upon. Here's a bucketful for them, and their parents and friends, indeed for all who miss that plangent, wry, hilarious voice, so early and sadly silenced in 1981.

Michael Parnell

* * *

Most of the editorial work for this volume was carried out by Michael Parnell, whose own voice was also 'early and sadly silenced', in 1991. A director of Seren Books, Michael Parnell was the biographer of Gwyn Thomas and an indefatigable editor of his work.

The publishers respectfully dedicate this book to the memory of Michael Parnell.

Mick Felton, Seren Books, November 1992.

The Face Of Our Jokes

My zone was the Rhondda. The place was flung together in a series of swift, large immigrations and, like that other great creation of multitudes on the move, the East Side of New York, it produced a vivid, bright and often outrageous humour.

Its position is significant. Unlike New York it is not the doorway to a continent. On the south, the junction of railway lines and roads transporting the stuff that fed the stockbrokers, factors and landowners of Cardiff. To the north, hills so deprived and forbidding they would be crossed only by dedicated athletes and aberrant absconders.

The fact that the place existed for coal and for coal alone struck a note of rich, black farce. The only Rhondda family to have a coat of arms made do with a sack and a bucket, the bucket hidden in the sack because we are a shy lot.

My father used to tell me of a coal-owner in a small way who was so mean he would not afford a cage to go up and down the shaft. He employed only bald men, and at the day's end these operators would stand patiently at the shaft's bottom while a rope descended with a sort of large leather washer attached. When this article had been fitted to the naked skull and had achieved a foolproof tightness, the worker was hauled up.

It was called the Sucker Pit. We believed it really existed and we still have a tendency to go round examining people's heads for washer-marks.

Housing was thrown up at a phenomenal rate, and dwellings tended to be small. If more than six people ate in the same kitchen one of them had to hold his plate out of the window, which accounts for my own taste for cool food.

Houses were in long, continuous, cottage-type strips. The only semi-detached houses were those that subsidence had caused to fall apart from the block. Walls were thin and life was loud. There were no secrets. Anybody found minding his own business was de-nounced as a freak or watched by the police. One of the reasons for the birth of our great choral tradition was that people in the ten houses to either side of you could hear exactly what you were saying, and having a group of people singing around you was the only way of ensuring a private conversation.

This meant a lot of frustration for the people in the ten houses on either side. So they joined in self-defence and before you knew it the whole street was giving out a strong beat.

Everywhere there was an air of jamboree. Neighbours, and some who were not neighbours, drifted in droves into each other's kit-chens. Some people got so tired of seeing total strangers ousting regular members of the family from the board, you never knew if a meal was going to start with broth or a blood test.

The poverty bit brought its own flavour to the humour of the valley: the family that ran a lottery to see which brother would get the middle cutlet of the sardine; the naïve young doctor prescribing oysters and champagne for an ailing miner and shocked when he found his patient having to make do on cockles and pop.

Thus the unforgettable councillor, Mark Harcombe, making his speech on the teeming economic difficulties of his day: "The efforts of capitalism to remedy the monetary evils of this area remind me of the doctor who was utterly unable to diagnose the state of a gravely ill patient. He gave the patient a pill.

'Will that cure him of what he's got, doctor?' asked the wife.

'I don't know. But it'll give him fits, and I'm first-class on fits.'"

And how many youngsters could find a trace of laughter on the man I heard in Hannah Street, Porth? He was passing a bank, the inside of which he was never likely to see unless he was whipped in there by a typhoon. "The trouble with a threepenny bit is, once you break into it it goes drib-drab." And there were houses where, if the mice took a nibble at the rent-book, they had to pay their share.

The funeral jokes flowed in a powerful tide. Two men sitting on a bench on Cemetery Road. One of them peers down the road. "Whose funeral is this then?" "Jones the Draper." "No!" "Well, It's not a rehearsal, anyway."

A neighbour goes to see the remains of an old friend before interment. On his way out of the house he turns to the widow. "Duw, he looks a treat." "Oh, yes, that last week in Llandudno did him a world of good."

The hastening hatchets of the industrialists, the builders, the fuel maniacs, made their contribution to the sardonic fun-book of the gulch. My father used to say that before the coming of the first coal-owners, a squirrel could proceed from Cardiff to the top of the Rhondda without once descending from the branches of the trees. A hundred years later you couldn't have got a squirrel up from Cardiff at all except under drugs, on the bus, or in pursuit of a very desirable lady squirrel.

Our rivers darkened by the hour. They were the only rivers where the water was so black and the people on the banks so friendly, the fish came out every five minutes for a song and a swill under the pump.

The rugby pitches on the hillsides were so steep one would often see both teams plunging down out of control, the referee just ahead of them, shouting for the law and trying to duck. A town could be hit on a Saturday afternoon by flying rugby players as parts of the Pacific are hit by cyclones.

The speech of the children could be movingly touched by sad absurdity. A brother of mine graduated in music after the first world war with special qualifications in piano and voice production. The times were against him and after a short while his career as a local professor of music ended, and he switched professional horses to become a sanitary inspector. From Sibelius to sewage in ten uneasy lessons and not unhappy to get there. One night, while he was still running his little academy, there was a knock on the door. It was a small girl from next door. "Please, Mr Emlyn, could I have my voice produced for the concert?"

"Of course, Nancy, of course. When is the concert?"

"Tomorrow night."

In our street were two fish and chip shops. A small lad would call in at the upper shop nightly with a bag containing a pennyworth of chips. He would help himself to a monsoon of vinegar, almost emptying the bottle. After a while the shopkeeper, a genial and tolerant man, peered over the counter and asked the boy, "Are those chips from in here?"

"No," said the boy, and with a smile as wide as China he spiked the guns of the shopkeeper's wrath with these words: "Mr Walton," he said, "there's nobody like you for vinegar. The vinegar down there in that other shop isn't a patch on yours. Thank you, Mr Walton."

The Silences Of Passion

In certain areas of life, I am told, love moves like a great and gifted fish from the current of one desire to the next. I have a strong feeling that I have been hanging around on the banks of the wrong streams, staring at the wrong seas. In the social contexts where my identity was fashioned, love, where it should have left a memorable radiance, created as often as not a mildewed quietness.

In any fairly ravaged industrial area, the face of love can be clobbered beyond recognition. Passionate liking is such an absurd and tenuous relationship it needs strong hints of grace and sophistication to provide it with a reasonable framework.

The early films provided us with many a shock as we saw the sheer floor-space in which the better-provided were allowed to develop their pre- and extra-marital antics. It created a fixed bitterness in young lovers who had a narrow choice to make between a back lane and a parlour in which an immovable uncle was tickling 'Abide With Me' up to a Sunday gloss on the harmonium.

In the South Wales of the '20s politics and religion twisted the arm of the libido with a consistent ferocity. We subsisted on speeches, sermons and hymns which declared that the only authentic love was the urge to unite socially with the rest of the species.

Sexual love came into it only to be denounced as an indecency, an irrelevance, a betraying and bathetic bit of farce, a sheltering in a stupid shadow, while the vast body of the army was advancing in light towards the uplands of total liberation. The nearest we got to the foot of Juliet's balcony was a demonstration. And we landed on the balcony itself only when we had some letter of scalding protest acknowledged on heat-proof vellum by the Prime Minister's secretary. Many a smooching amorist was dragged from a protective doorway by a father beating him half to death with a handful of knotted pamphlets.

Love needs an oxygen of confidence and when one has known an ambience of grotesque indignity one approaches personal love as warily as one would a gaol-break. The adulterers I recall from my childhood were few, although I admit that I was not at that time watching out for them. The ones who were brought to my attention by relatives anxious to point out to me in a cautionary way the various paths to hell were jolly, roaring outlaws, not giving the sliver of a damn for their shattered respectability, and defying the pious to apply to them the execution by dog, stone or exile prescribed in the rougher pages of the Old Testament. They were, too, heavily dependent on drink for their excesses and in days of slump tended to crawl back into an autumnal restraint, and the places where extra-mural love throve, like the warmed wall of the old steam-fan and the back of the dance-hall, fell silent.

We followed these sinners about with praise, encouragement and building foods. They and the revivalists were the only people whose signatures we sought, thinking that in handwriting might be some clue to success.

From the numberless chapels which had splintered off from the Established Church flew many fragments of further dissent. These new persuasions settled themselves in small huts, usually on the moorland fringe of the town. The religious idiom in these places was much more passionately assertive and individual than in the conventional temples. I suppose starting up a new sect is classically a crypto-sexual act, for it is simply a desire to introduce some sensational novelty into one's relations with others. One is looking for a new and astonishing posture, a new chime of echoes for a voice maddeningly muffled.

I did a fair amount of research into these breakaway conventicles, usually on winter nights when sensual fervour ran thin. The sectaries reached a high degree of excitement. They did not favour long, set statements by a chosen preacher or hymns decorously sung. Their fancy ran to accordions, to dancing of a stamping kind, and self-revelations delivered in gibberish and a half-delirium. If the drug coca had been cultivable in those hills I would say that they had stumbled across a fair plantation of it.

My envy of them had edges of unforgettable anguish. Their ecstasy would move swiftly from the mystical to the sexual. The accordian would keep playing, because musicians of this type get their own kinds of satisfaction which are not explicable in terms of other love techniques. It must have something to do with those straps and a swiftly manipulable keyboard. But many couples would leave the hut, yap up in joy at the frost-bright stars, canter up into the darkness of the hillside, then find bliss disperse abruptly as their bodies touched the freezing surface of the moor.

We wished them well, for they appeared to have reached a superb synthesis of the two passions we most admired, preaching and kissing. And the sight of their slow, sad progression from the heights back down to the blinking censure of the valley bed's streets led us to the discovery of one of our first principles, that the levels of heat on this earth are disastrously and inextricably uneven.

In the lives of many of the women in that time there must have been caves of yearning. Men whose maturing was too often a simple rejection of tenderness, over-large broods of children, tormented by a lack of space and calories into muttering insurrection, hutch-houses where a wish for privacy passed as something sinister, a symptom of contempt or eccentricity, these things did a perfect Jack the Ripper job on more women than even Jack ever dreamed of. Death could often be seen backing in shame from such a lack of fulfilment.

On to the lives of such women the reasoning of demagogues and revivalists fell like an appeasing dew: their candent perorations warmed like brandy. The great revivalists came to revive something more than a limping theology. At their best they relieved more sieges of coldness than the gulf stream. They shattered silences that threatened to become funereal. They set lights swinging in dreams that had slipped betimes into a penultimate shroud.

I am thinking of one such wizard who lived well into my own lifetime. During one summer, when he was in his middle twenties and supremely handsome after the fashion of Henry Ainley, he burst forth from some Calvinistic Death Valley in the far Welsh west, his eyes mesmeric with conviction, his tongue a thunderclap of sonorous hallelujahs. Every crouching heart in the land rose in a full ecstasy of response. Men paddled into the harbour of salvation after years on a broad lagoon of booze. Four members of the local quoits team, athletes of depravity, confessed their sins publicly and asked for admission into the orbit of grace. The whole audience wept as they saw these scamps sob and foreswear quoits, sex, ale and the glee-group. They lapsed that very night, somewhere between the chapel and their homes, lured into a sawdust bar by some voter who had big gambling money involved in a quoits contest which the four converts stood a chance of winning.

But for the women it was a more serious thing. Their need for beauty, which a man can drown in a pint or stiffle with a jest, is in them organic and abidingly disquieting. For them our revivalist was a combination of Valentino and Lloyd George; Latin frankness set squarely in the midst of a hymn-singing and Radical democracy. The less timid went down to his enchantment like skittles. The pulpit on which he stood was less like a lectern than a protective screen. He spoke of the sun of warmth and love that was shortly to rise over the stricken tundra of their days. The brilliance of his innovations exploded with blinding force between them and the image of the muffled rocks and belted bellies of their shuffling and beer-logged mates.

There was an occasion when he was found in a fern-bed in flagrant delight with one of his young worshippers. It was a great mistake. When one is stroking a communal libido it is tactless to particularise. That evening, a whole army of enraged lovers assembled in the chapel and a mood of lynching was in the air. The deacons refused to take any part in the opening hymns. Two sidesmen soaped the rope. Two hundred pairs of female eyes did not leave his blushing face. He dangled from the grudge they bore him. We small ones in the gallery heard dreams topple and hit the ground so hard we wondered if it was just life again or a fresh onset of subsidence.

The revivalist stood up for his sermon. This, we thought, was one torero who would gladly ask the bull to get on with it. He opened his arms and leaned towards us. He said nothing. He was inviting us to brood upon all the places in the lives of men and women where love needed to go and, sometimes, inscrutably went. We brooded. Our spirits went towards him like lemmings, fascinated by the cliffs of his confessed anguish. He began, softly, to conjugate the verb 'to love' in Welsh and English. His voice had a quite unearthly timbre and reach. The precentor, a megalomaniac and a hard man to stop when he felt the mood was with him, began to hum one of our lovelier songs of lamentation. At least three women left the place, weeping, to mark the falling from the sky of yet another love.

At the end of that summer the revivalist, his larynx and most of the rest of him spent, retired into private life. He took with him a curious seraglio, a group of exquisite hand-maidens, his favourite gospel-singers. And he left behind him a land that he had come to salve and left even more scarred and apprehensive than it had been before.

I fancied the revivalist line myself. Indeed I fancied anything that would make me a magisterial and admirable fellow, letting off storms of compassion in the female breast, flanked by women groaning for a fresh sound, sight and touch of me. I practised a few perorations in the kitchen and thought I was doing fairly well until my brothers found a soporific herb and three wrestling grips that kept me out for the count for days on end. Also, my faith withered, and most of my carnal urges with it.

For me, Spurgeon dropped out of sight at about the same time as Casanova. On a blazing day in 1924 I was bitten by a rabid student of Bradlaugh who was crawling about in the Free Thought section of the Library and Institute. I lost my urge to preach and impress my name and wishes on the melting hearts of women.

Which is a pity, for I too can conjugate the verb "to love" in Welsh and English. And Spanish, too, if the thing ever went on tour.

Down With The Libido

Sex has always seemed to come between me and enjoyment. There was the time when it cut short my career as a chess wizard. It happened when I was about thirteen. Out of the dusk of my childhood bats of a new sensibility were flying, keeping me on high levels of torment. I had been a noisy child. I had a feeling that once I had done with the antics of puberty my attitudes would be intemperate, possibly violent.

I wanted quietness. I had had enough of loud emotionalism. Even at that age my life had been scarred by an excessive evangelism. I had sung so many songs warning people against adultery and drink that several voters, planning a plunge into delirium and betrayal, would come to me and ask permission. I had appeared in many juvenile missionary sketches as a dissident native, playing hell with economic order and moral law in our various colonies, swigging palm wine and driving the Missionary League out of its mind. The pattern of the sketches was rigid. At the end I was mauled by a puma, poisoned by one of my own darts, or I might break my neck or leg storming the missionary's stockade. The missionary would cure me and put me on the right, pliant, ideological path. I would swear off drink, pamphlets, oratory, accept a motherly kiss from the missionary's wife and embrace a working compromise with the Church of England and the Raj.

I did this so often that a local group of direct-action Marxists, convinced that I was castrating the whole impulse towards colonial freedom, threatened to sprinkle my Welsh-cakes with white-lead. They did not do so. Not that they lacked the will or the white-lead. It was just that interfering with Welsh-cakes was supposed to invite bad luck.

And in all these sketches and other types of moralising joust to which I was a party, there would be a girl to whom, with terrible impotence, I would give my heart, as the phrase was. Each one was invariably similar to the one before: the face, flattish, dark and sad, throwback to some half-remembered Deirdre, unless all the girls just happened to look like that.

These pressures played havoc with my academic work. My mind slowed down to such a crawl that at least three teachers, driven by zeal to come too close, tripped over it and did themselves a hurt. They did not regard me as a distracted clown trying to pick up the fragments of his own true self from the fox-holes of a private hell. They wrote me off as a simple dunce. That hurt my pride and landed me in a bog of angry embarrassment that has never really dried out.

I failed totally in all pursuits that called for coolness and acuity. Sexual obsession never fails to ruin one in any subject that calls for great powers of careful analysis. Love has no interest in constituent parts, either of structure or purpose. Would you have found Pascal or Newton hanging around the scarlet areas of life and chasing about after girls? No; and by the same token you would not have found me fainting with love over an equation or teasing a further secret out of some arid triangle. Sex clobbers clarity, which would have made me dislike it even more did we not live in a society that offers so little worthy of appraisal with unfogged eyes.

So, at thirteen I was exhausted, in retreat, shaken half to death by the souring betrayals of public performance and private desire. I wished to hide my expression of puzzled penitence with a wig made of hair salvaged from the manes of Savonarola and Knox, poor headgear by any standard. I ordered all winds to drop and looked for escape roads, difficult to find before one has touched those serious delinquencies that bring society pressing helpful fingers into the middle of one's spine.

My attention was caught by a group of boys in the sixth form some three or four years my senior. They were distinctive. They were quietly, tidily dressed as if on their way to some eternal vestry, and aloof from the ogling, smoking and blasphemy that ran like leopard's stripes down the school's body. I watched these boys with admiration and determined to be their acolyte.

They went each evening to the Miners' Welfare Hall and played chess in the appropriate room. The over-large families and congested kitchens and parlours of the period meant that one had to stun a few people to get the patch of immobile space that a chessboard calls for. Besides, in the Welfare Hall one never saw girls.

It was clear to me that whatever contract of nerve and blood keeps sex going, these chess players had pulled out of it. They rarely spoke. They had told life to button everything, including the lip, and they would move smoothly from college into some strict corner of a Carthusian house. They were officially listed as the Welfare Hall Junior Chess Team. Their prim, asexual approach was endorsed and praised by all the local Puritans who wanted to see the libido dragged, gagged and helpless, through the ashes.

At first they did not fancy my presence. It got on their nerves to find me perpetually at their side looking grateful, delighted, keen or just impassive with a touch of menace, which is a look much called for in chess. The older users of the room wanted no part of me. They knew me only as a visiting Pathan, who had sometimes come nipping into the room, shouting, singing, brawling with my mates, collecting jokes of a revealing kind and upsetting some very astute players who were perfecting ploys that would rout the Russians and sharpen the intellectual edge of Welsh nonconformity, then very blunt.

I wanted to be admitted at once into the Chess mystery. The game made no sense to me. It never does, I am told, to the briskly sensual. This was not helped by the sixth formers who told me to watch and wait. I wanted to be lashing out with rooks and besieging bishops. But the boys had their programme for me fixed. They had spotted me as a disordered element, a lad bold with his eyes in the face of girls, a vocalising amorist of bronze effrontery, ardent in his flesh on all fronts, in chapel services, in concerts and the town square, a hub of lust before the buses came along to make the art of spotting and pursuit less easy.

Watch and wait, said the Junior Chess Team. Before the summer was done they would reveal every wrinkle of chess craft to me. They would make me a master, the first adolescent to have Alekhine crouching under the table, a checkmating sage purged of every untidy urge and headed for a serene and sexless maturity.

They did not keep a single promise. They never admitted me to a game. That was the summer of the carnivals. These carnivals were large, fancy-dress affairs meant to help us over a sandy patch in a year of crisis. A large element in the carnivals was the category of 'Individual Characters'. The clothes of these performers were sketchy. One man appeared in three different carnivals as Caractacus, Hereward the Wake and Owen Glyndwr, without altering a stitch of his original costume.

A committee man would patrol, the flanks of the carnival throwing in notes to clarify the appearance of excessively vague impersonators. They would point to a man in some hybrid outfit who could quite easily have been either walking in his sleep or calling on behalf of the Water Board. "Beau Geste", the committee man would say. "You would have spotted him for Beau in a flash but he lost his képi when he nipped out for a pint in the Orb back there."

Sex rose over the place like a great moon. Day after day broke in brilliant heat. The hillsides were like the walls of a vast Venusberg. Women normally recessive emerged with a wish to flaunt and inflame. Deacons fled, the young simmered, the Sunday schools lost colour and stayed in pallid silences on the sidelines.

The queen of these revels was a girl called Josette Jaynes. She impersonated Carmen and she played every trick in the Andalusian pack. Her costume was based on the turnout she had studied on various Carmens in the local cinema. It was a cinema where, between an ill-aimed projector and a defiance of ventilation, it was impossible to observe anything with accuracy. She wore a gardenful of flowers in her hair and carried a rose in her mouth. She was aware of the excitement she caused in the watching men and boys and this, in turn, excited her. She grasped the rose so tightly between her teeth the juice of its stem gathered on her chin. The beckoning power of this simple act of chewing was immense. And the movement of her body when she hitched the crimson shawl more firmly round her shoulders sent sensitive men hurtling into our river, the Moody, which came from the mountains and was always cool.

Josette's father was a butcher and fiercely jealous of Josette's good name. He would confront every new arrival in the queue of her admirers, produce from an inside pocket a butcher's knife of the shorter type, and tell the lover to think it over.

As the summer went on my companions in the chess-room dropped away. One by one they fell in love with Josette, who found them, as new specimens, fascinating. They forsook chess and all serious mental exercise. They were chased occasionally and threatened with cold steel by Josette's father, and that gave them another reason to shake and fall. Even I, at thirteen, was a goner for Josette, but, between meditation, my dreams of chess mastery and a sedative preparation made of syrup and sulphur, managed to keep it under control.

I waited for my chess-playing friends to return to sanity, to become my gurus in a long reign of calm. They never did. The carnivals came to an end. Josette retired, the only pseudo-Carmen to eat her own weight in roses and seduce an entire chess team.

The following winter I returned to public singing, and that was another watershed experience. I was the alto soloist in a curious item written by a local man. I was supposed to be an orphaned boy, bereaved by some ghastly disaster connected with coal, and telling of his plight in bitter words. I was surrounded by the mourning mothers of the world, a ladies' choir, all offering me comfort. They stood around me, very close. They were all in full boom and bloom. They wore white satin blouses, which, when they leaned forward in some climax of pity, sometimes touched my head. It was too much. Between that voluptuousness and a suit against which my growing body strained, and a series of badly carpentered and sloping stages, I kept going off key. My desires never again got back onto an even keel.

Life never returned to the level of that summer and winter. When ripeness came I made short and foolish trips between tips of ashen disappointment. As with chess, so with sex; I never mastered the rules, never really saw the point. Sex has remained a banality in fact and a nuisance in fiction.

The Hard Word

There is no sight that more readily flattens ale and gelds delight than that of a bar full of afternoon drinkers bewitched by television racing. For them, the sounds that roar from the set, the commentator mounting to a supersonic gibber, the punters urging on the nags, are the strongest wine in life.

Neither love nor patriotism can exert so continuous a grip on men and women as the habit which makes a man pick up his form sheet each morning to find the fancy on which his bet will go. They are, in a sense, the lucky ones, for there are few things of indestructible interest. The eyes grow weary of print, pictures that once bewitched us lose their sharpness, the loveliness of nature grows less desirable as the body begins to buckle under the strain of tiredness and rain. A blur of tedium falls at last upon the most hallowed music. Don Juan, the compulsive amorist, finds a point where the barbed wire of malice and disgust threads through his tangled affairs. Even the most exhilarated pickpocket must one day feel his hand disgraced by entry into so many other people's clothes, and he will wish that he had taken up woodwork. But the bettor has a phobia which seemingly never palls. Every day on which horses set forth from their starting posts will bring him face to face with high drama. His gambling may hurt his pocket but it will expose his body to no hazard unless he tries to welsh on a slippery surface. His mind, spinning in its daily welter of guesses, forecasts and fetishes, is free from the issues that plague and erode the minds of the more earnest.

I never came anywhere near to entering this charmed and witless circle. I would be more at ease among Martians than with an average group of racing people. Horses I love when they are standing still. In movement they make me feel threatened. The same goes for bookmakers.

My whole childhood was a cautionary tale against gambling. One of my teachers, a secret gambler and very mean, I suspect, would put the occasional shilling on a horse and invariably lose because he had that unshakable belief in outsiders which is one of the most endearing things about the teaching profession. After each defeat he would come back to the classroom, his eyes glazed with shock, his posture dramatically bent by disgust at his weakness and rage at having dented his savings. He would then give us a series of readings from Dickens's *The Old Curiosity Shop* in which Nell's grandfather progressively crucifies himself on the cross of his gaming fever. The teacher read well. He hung all his own frustrations around the grandfather's neck, and a heavy wreath he made of it. We were solidly behind Nell and if we ever spotted a bookmaker on the street we would stand close together and treat him to a dark, collective frown.

Today in places like South Wales we have casinos. Cosy places, subtly lit, with croupiers as suave and sharp-faced as any we ever saw in the cinema. A new idiom of gambling has emerged. It is commonplace to stand in a bar and hear one of the sage young dogs admit to having dropped fifty at chemmy. The new folly is the face of the new affluence. All the high tides of denunciation from Puritans and nay-sayers will not restore gambling to the rather furtive, outlawed rate it had been before the war. In my youth it had a most raffish and undesirable look about it. It was an activity of little comfort. One would see groups of gamblers on the hilltops crouching low in the ferns to avoid the eyes of the law, and all around converging trails of blue, which were policemen closing in for the swoop. One of our hobbies was raising a hullabaloo to give the trespassers a chance to leg it back down the valley before the school could be apprehended.

Their favourite game was pontoon, a simple exercise that scarcely dusted the mind and allowed a quick turnover of decisions, losses and gains. You could tell these gamblers in after years, for that business of crouching to keep out of sight laid a permanent mark on them, and they played with their cards so close to the chest that their waistcoats often bore the stigma of an entire pack.

The stakes for which they played were tiny. Pennies and even matches were the general currency. They never stood a chance of plunging into the total and terrifying ruin that awaited Nell's grandfather or a legendary character who lived in our street, a man who had developed reckless habits during a short spell as a silver miner in Colorado. On his return he was an inveterate gambler and at least four chapels raised a demand that he be deported back to the Comstock Lode. In one day, it was said, he laid down as stakes, in a two-day poker game, the little transport company he had started and the house in which he lived with his wife and four children. He lost the company and the home, and he became very quiet and said he would devote his life henceforth to temperance, thrift and truth. He even admitted he had never been anywhere near Colorado.

Of racing tracks in my zone we had a few. I recall a group of reactionary Corinthians eager to lessen the radical earnestness of the local Left. They tried to establish a horse-racing track. It was a rudimentary affair. The course was so uneven and ill-fenced, the jockeys were scattered like chaff and the horses made off in so many different directions that what started as a tight little gallop finished as a nationwide search.

There was a dog-track in my town and it was there I made my second and last bet. My first bet was a shilling on a dog called Trigo. I had been tempted into this venture by sheer pedantry. I knew that 'trigo' was the Spanish for wheat and there was also a man called trigo who was a well-known lecherous Spanish novelist, and this type of writer often brings luck. Trigo won. The last bet was on a black dog. I was in a cautious mood that evening. The triumph of Trigo had not made me reckless. It had won, but the man whom I had deposited the bet had not paid up. He had been last seen footing it through Lydney with a baying posse of punters at his heels. But my confidence grew as I watched those dogs. For in all the first five races a black dog won. I asked if there was a black dog in the sixth race. There was. I found a sixpence and sought a bookmaker. I looked for the least fit bookmaker on the field, the one least likely to beat an unscrupulous retreat with my loot. The race began. Five dogs came shooting from the traps like bullets. The last dog to emerge was jet black. He took a few steps, stopped, looked around with profound Byronic gloom, then ambled back into the trap, probably to announce his forthcoming marriage to the electric hare.

Gambling does not admit of doubt. There are, of course, those who rig the odds. There are astonishing people who predetermine a horse's form by shooting it full of ciston oil, a substance once used for the relatively homely tasks of purging constipated elephants and drugging drunken or refractory sailors. There are those inscrutable operators whose both sleeves have a lining of aces. People like

Damon Runyon's 'The Brain', of whom it was said: "If this guy comes up to you and says he has a pack of cards which, for a small wager, will squirt apple-juice in your ear, do not accept the wager or you will end up with an earful of apple-juice."

But the great army of gamblers have certainty without reason. They will prepare to wager the moon on a horse they have never seen. The more scientific will follow up certain hints from the *Breeder' Guide* or the *Punters' Annual*. But in the main it will be the name, an association with one's place of origin, a friend, or merely a pleasing run of syllables. We had a neighbour who worked out a system of forecasts which would, he was convinced, land him with the biggest betting coup since Lord George Bentinck who, in 1843, had £150,000 riding on a horse, Gaper, in the Derby. This neighbour of ours was called Williams the Weights and his system hinged on some correlation between the weight of the jockey and the weight of the horse. The quality of the tap-water in the neighbourhood of the race-course also came into it somewhere. Williams the Weights never, to my knowledge, won. After each defeat he would look shrewder than ever, send a wire off to the jockey telling him to weigh again. A similar cable went off to the horse, with a footnote to the Borough Engineer telling him to change the tap-water. But Williams the Weights never achieved his dream of challenging the reign of the late Prince Monolulu.

The Walking Compulsion

As a walker I overdid it from the start. We were a large family in a small house and there was heavy congestion in the bedrooms. There was general relief when it was learned in my earliest childhood that I was a sleepwalker. At the drop of a dream I would be afoot and off, sleeping like a rock, moving through doors as fluently as the noted burglar Springheel Jack, clad in a rough shift and humming patriotic songs, and stumbling into covens of local witches, all earthbound, being too houseproud to use their brooms for anything as pointless as flight. I also upset many late revellers, who advised my parents either to chain me up or persuade me, if my somnambulism persisted, to cut out the humming part of my routine which, they said, was eerie.

I look back upon the experience with regret. It was the only physical movement I have ever undertaken without a sense of gripping terror, the only travelling I have ever done without mordant anxiety. I have often wondered about the motivation of those nightly walks. One of my brothers, a subtle opportunist and a sleeping companion in that Asiatic phase of our lives, had a certain hypnotic knack, and I would not put it past him to have cast some sort of mesmeric spell over my mind at the first onset of slumber, not merely urging me to get up and start moving but directing me into all those corners of the village where my appearance in a shift and singing withal would cause the greatest perturbation. It left him with a more viable slice of the bed. There is a general agreement that the distances involved in those sleeping rambles account for the chronic fatigue which has been my shadow ever since.

I never used transport to or from either of the two schools I attended. The primary school was just the length of a back lane away, but getting there could involve a lot of time and activity. The lane seemed always full of boys lurking in doorways and as ready as Pathans to launch an attack. These boys lived in an idiom of generalised malice, dealing no more than one stunning blow before taking flight. One of the few benefits of the great hunger that was shortly to beset the region was that it made these performers more torpid in their approach to their neighbours.

The school's headmaster was a fiery and explosive man, and we would often walk five or six times around the block to delay the moment when we would see his face burst into a military bellow. His being hinged on two things. Having missed service in the Great War he was a sergeant-major manqué. He had a huge, inaccurate baritone voice, which had baulked him justly out of his wish to lead the singing in the chapel. He stropped both phobias into lasting sharpness on our terrified backs. If our singing in the morning assembly struck him as rough he would lead us out into the yard and march us endlessly around. At the end of each minute, with a roar like massed cannon, he would urge us to a quicker tempo. He told us to ignore pupils who fell flat on their faces with vertigo. He kept us at it until he thought our lungs were limber enough for another tilt at the hymnal.

The yard had high, sombre walls which hung a permanent penitentiary fringe on my thoughts. Being whirled as part of a human roulette wheel beneath those grey cliffs has given to most of my dreams a viciously circular and panting quality. At the end of the exercise he would lead us back into the school. Often he would pause at the top of the steps, flag us to a halt, and say: "This morning we marched on Kabul." Psychologically the man was eternally trotting behind Lord Roberts and we would not have worked our calf-muscles to a greater tightness if he had been thrusting us up and down genuine Afghan slopes. Given a few more years of rule he would, one punch-drunk morning, press on through the Hindu Kush and take Russia.

The walk to the County School was another matter. It involved a long walk downhill and an equally long walk uphill and by the end of the second year I was walking with a kind of Peruvian obliquity, riding the punch of the killing gradients. The name of the approach avenue to the school was Cemetery Road and that slowed me down considerably. I arrived late at school so often the County Council sent an envoy to explain what the school's official hours were.

Floods were a help. At the confluence of the two valleys we had the touchiest set of rivers in Britain. After a spell of rain, and nature was steady and sullen in that direction, the hillsides would be slashed by thousands of fractious little streams and the citizens on the lower slopes would be urged by gum-booted criers to take to the boats or the hills. Our normal approach to Cemetery Road would be cut off and we were advised by the authorities to find alternative routes. We would not have made heavier weather of the Great Ice Barrier. We wandered about like Bedouin, creating mirages of impassable water in places that were dry as a cork. We were accoutred well for this task. We had all obtained, by means that are still not clear, sets of tall, waterproof gaiters, and we made our interminable tour of the back lanes looking like a gaggle of small, sinister bishops. The gaiters gave us reassurance. We kept them on for weeks after the monsoon had cried its last eyes out. When the Council made a system of conduits that kept the rivers calm and predictable we lost a whole hint of paradise.

Walking scarred the years of my early manhood. In my part of the valley about the only thing that was working was my thyroid gland and it was doing that to excess. Up-rushes of toxins got me the presidency of the manic-depressive lodge and planted in me a set of compulsions that made me, in all contexts, worth watching. One of them was the compulsion to walk. In the middle of a sentence or a meal I would, without one word of explanation or gesture of apology, leave the company and begin a walk at formidable speed up the hillside and over the moorland. People seeing me vanish in this fashion with such urgency, with such a look of atrabilious strain on my face, would often follow me in large groups, thinking that I had just received some apocalyptic message and was leaving the valley the hard way.

Lovely as the hilltops were, there was not a single note of delight in those lonely and distracted marches. They were a total nightmare. I perspired like a fever victim and jabbered alternately with sheep and the Erl King. The end of the movement would be blackout and collapse. One of the few regular bits of betting in the zone was on where they'd find me next. I understand now that the point of all this frenetic exercise was an instinctive attempt to dilute or expel the juices of that wretched gland.

There was also a recurrence of night-walking at this period. But there was no element of somnambulism in this. Mental stimulation, as the thyroxine rose in the well, made sleep impossible. The complaint made me horribly eloquent and it was always easy to persuade some group of friends to come with me on a huge walk during the hours after midnight. I wore out whole rafts of acquaintances and it has been claimed that my need to recruit companions for these safaris through the hours of darkness accounted for as much migration from the area as our demented economic system itself.

This phase added a new dimension of daftness to our ordinary fare. We were constantly flashed at by policemen's lanterns. We were reproached by people crouched over their garden walls listening to various off-beat night-birds competing with the regional lust for oratorio, or gathering healing simples, or planting seed in the pre-dawn hush in some favourable quarter of the moon.

Always I seemed to be walking away from something. Then the tensions eased. My thyroid married and either settled down or emigrated. Bemusement at having survived through the drizzling days and quaking midnights to achieve the age of thirty bred a splendid indifference and an end to the need to be muttering on mountain tops about all mankind. And the pay-off was one particularly pensive stroll when I was hurled through a hedge by a blue Mercedes, my only link with that type of motoring.

Now when I walk at all I see all the things I used to walk away from marching towards me from the opposite direction. I stand quite still to delay the shock of encounter.

GROWING UP IN MEADOW PROSPECT

1
Brotherly Love

The acoustics of childhood are terrible. The basic failure to give or receive messages up to the age of twelve accounts for most of the bewilderment that keeps many faces rigid from then to the grave. Most of what a child hears is muffled or deplorable. That he assembles the elements of some kind of sanity before it gets time for manhood is the most formidable bit of craftsmanship in our experiences. That most of the sanity is not shaken off the plate again before the age of thirty is due only to the fact that we learn to keep very still.

According to the form-book I should have been well placed in this business of projecting myself in childhood, of establishing the sort of identity with which I could feel blithe and secure. Looking forward shrewdly at the age of three I would have said that I was the child most likely to receive every type of love and devotion listed in the child welfare manuals. It may have turned out that way. If so, someone must have been using a torn copy of the manual or reading in a poor light.

According to tradition and most fiction, the youngest of twelve children and the eighth of eight brothers can afford to be smug. He is the Benjamin, the chubby mascot on whom the distilled affection of all his elders is showered, over whom the fanatical love of his brothers is laid like a shield. I must have stood in the wrong shower, and there was something wrong about that shield too. I was chubby all right, but from that moment on the tradition dropped down dead. Either they had not heard of mascots or the name Benjamin had died on the wind.

Happiness is largely a matter of timing, of expert communication. The great lump of our malaise is made up of good and loving intentions that were put on the wrong train and landed at the wrong moment. At timing, as an earthly art, I was never more than a Martian. Often my brothers would have a close harmony session in the kitchen during which I would be boomed out of countenance and told to pipe down because my treble was too piercing. The singing done, the table would be laid for supper. My brothers, sung out, would sit in silence. I would feel an urge to show my kinship with them and give out with the loudest hymn or carol I knew. This would always turn out to be the one song able to give toothache to growing Celts in a small room with cutlery exposed. Either I was chased off to bed or fitted with a rough cosy of pillows. If I tried spinning a top it was usually within earshot of a brother who was writing an essay on the slave trade, and was allergic to the sound of whipping. If a brother was entertaining a sweetheart in the front room this was the moment I would choose to recruit a dozen friends to play 'Bomberino' to impress the sweetheart with what a gay lot we were. This bomberino is a game where half the players form a sort of crouching crocodile against a wall and the remaining players leap as high up the crocodile as they can. I played this game against the outer wall of the front room. We played it violently with loud shouting to induce a mood of summer abandon in the lovers within. I did not know it at the time but the game put the whole house, especially the front room, in jeopardy. The inner wall would flake, the piano-lid would be dislodged, and every leap produced a thud so disconcerting that we would have sent Cellini, at his most ardent, back to his silver work. Always the wrong foot in the wrong place. Every time I whistled up into a blue sky I got thunder back for my trouble.

Once, after a long tour of the Book of Genesis in the Sunday School, I told them the story of Jacob, Joseph and Benjamin. I explained to them how Benjamin, the youngest, had been beloved by his brothers, but they missed this part because my father was in the front room rehearsing his glee group and shaking the tiles off with the volume. Then I told them how Joseph's brothers had taken him to the vale of Dotham and left him to die in a pit. They got this part very plain and they asked me how I was fixed for a stroll on the following Saturday to a part of the mountain that was full of fissures.

So I ceased trying to co-exist, to assuage. I would wait for their every moment of disquietude and squat on it like a waiting vulture. If, chafing at the approach of some important date, a shirt would ravel, a lace would break, or if they appeared for the first time in some adult absurdity like a wing collar and bow-tie, I would follow them around staring until I felt myself nibbling at the last morsel of their assurance. Or I would make a remark meant to sting or enrage. And I must say that within the vocabulary limit of a juvenile I could be as noxiously sub-acid as the uninvited fringe of a Royal garden party. Quite often I could have purchased security, if not happiness, if I had kept my mouth shut for ten seconds. But I had to communicate. And before the last word was out, I was pelting away from the wrath to come.

They fixed finally on a form of punishment that would inflict maximum indignity on me and the least wear and tear on them. They would fling me into the recess below the stairs. This place was roughly equivalent to what, I believe, they call in American gaols 'the hole.' It had a strong door bolted from the outside. When the door was closed it was as dark as the underside of a dungeon, as airless as the bed of the sea. And I was the boy who knew. I was a freeman of that borough. The place was full of ancient clothes that no one would accept the acrid duty of throwing out. And there were some potatoes in a far corner stored there in reply to a threatened famine of long before. They didn't help.

Normally I could depend on making my first trip into this crypt about 5 p.m. following a round of impertinence at the tea-table after seeing my hand beaten time and again to the sandwich plate by fingers longer and stronger than mine. I would rage in the darkness, bang my hands, fling myself against the door and hurl abuse at my gaolers in ways that have not been bettered in any prison drama. But the only reaction that came from the kitchen was a sound of tremendous eating and happy laughter as the brethren noted what a better place the kitchen was without me. Some of my assaults on the door were muffled by the curtain of old coats that had been hanging there since they were last used as a disguise on a toll-gate burning job in 1837. But they cut down on possible bruising so I did not bother to unhook them. Sometimes I would fall tired and sit on the floor, thinking of other notable convicts. My all-time favourite was Edmond Dantès whose story had been read to me fitfully by my father in the hour before opening time. He had a way of constantly looking at the clock while reading, and he would often flick over a page. For close on a year and a half he kept Dantès and myself on the hop. I brooded often on Dantès as a tunneller. But any tunnelling from that calaboòse would have led me straight into the hands of those who would regard it as a birthday treat to put me back there. When they let me out I would behave with a cunning submissiveness, producing a few tears and asking gentle questions about the crafts and hobbies then popular with the various members of the family. The answers to those queries got shorter as the questioner began to suspect that I was planning some looting action against their stock of fretwork, cork-work, sheet-music or modelling clay. It usually took me about fifteen minutes to assemble the materials for a fresh trip to the chokey.

The day I beat my own record was the wettest day in a short, drenched summer. It was the day chosen for the Sunday School outing. I was up about five and went coursing up and down the hillside street, shaking my fist at the sky and explaining to anyone I could see through the thick mist and rain that all these phenomena were the augurs of a heat wave. I was violently clipped twice by people startled at hearing someone awake and prophesying at that hour in the morning, and denounced once as being either a satirist or the sectary who was laying on this sort of weather on behalf of an opposed denomination.

I got back to the house to breakfast and dress. I was wet and fractious. They told me that in view of the weather and the world's general air of mourning, I could leave my bucket and spade at home and wear my new overcoat. The bucket and spade sanction I could ride because my urge to dig and shovel had never ripened. But I stuck at the coat. It was a black article, bought deliberately large to allow for growth, and they had had their eyes fixed well beyond puberty. If I ever grew out of that thing it would be by way of one of the sleeves. It came down to my boots and the velvet collar stood a clear four inches from the back of my neck as if trying to work out our relationship. I told them they'd see me dead before I'd wear a coat of that sort on a Sunday School treat. They thought seriously about that for a minute or two. They told me that either I would go to Barry with the overcoat or into the cwtch without it. I tried the coat on. I looked in the mirror. I was like the senior priest in some sullen brotherhood. I took the coat off, opened the door of the cwtch and latched it behind me. I did not bang my fists or protest. I sat

instantly on the floor and told the surrounding shadows that com-
pared with me Dantès had been on Butlin territory.

I was released under the hour. They were worried that I might
have crept into the corner where the ancient potatoes mouldered
and committed a quiet hara-kiri just to embarrass them. They also
wanted me to help them in diverting a mountain stream which had
broken loose from its banks and was headed straight for the kitchen
— a Mississippi manoeuvre that happened about fourteen times a
year. I worked listlessly with the sandbags, for in those moods I was
with the stream. When I finished I started on a brisk round of social
service. I stood outside the room where one brother was rehearsing
'It is enough' from Elijah, a piece of oratorio that really put the
helmet on a rainy day, and kept up a distracting buzzing sound
which suggested that Elijah might be talking back. Then I deflated
the rugby ball of the brother who had just been made captain of the
village's junior fifteen. From there I went on to pouring glue over
the clay of the brother who was trying to add sculpture as an extra
tassel to the Celtic fringe. When these deeds were uncovered I was
in and out of the hole like a piston.

The last trip was at half past seven. My eldest brother was putting
on his tie, a very long black one crochetted for him by his girl. She
must have measured his torso with a loose tape or become bemused
by the play of the needles. It was long enough to hinder walking. I
stared at it and started on the kind of corrosive banter that was my
standard cry in the darkness of the time. I asked him if he was
headed for a wooing or a hanging. He advanced on me with the tie
strongly noosed for action. Then he changed his mind and threw
me into the cwch. When he left the house the place was empty and
silent. I was in for a spell. I arranged my back comfortably against
the wall and told Surajah Dowla to move up.

Logically I should have stayed there until about ten. But my father
had had a strange evening at the club and had been thrown out of
his routine. He had lost two arguments and one game of cribbage
and had failed to make the bill on the annual concert with a
recitation he had written himself about John Lee, the man they
could not hang, a man and topic that so obsessed him that I spent
two clear years of my childhood thinking he was Lee, hiding his
identity and stroking his neck. He had also ran across a few copies
of the Salvation Army weekly *The War Cry* which contained some
of the sharpest things the Army had ever said about drink and

neglectful parents. He walked home a good hour before time with big, sad apocalyptic thoughts trailing about him. He came into the kitchen. I was half asleep in the crypt and just vaguely stirring. He kicked the wainscoting and shouted to the mice to clear off before they ran into cats or poison. I raised myself above the mouse-level with a few clear shouts. My father let me out. The sight of me set off gushers of pity. He led me on to the flagged area we called the 'back paving.' He pointed to the sky. Its lower regions were a brilliant crimson with reflections from the great steel ovens being tapped at Merthyr three or four mountains to the north. The sense of doom, triggered off by his brush with failure and remorse in the club, became passionate in my father. He pointed at the scarlet flickers. "Do you know what they mean?" he said "No." I had not heard about the steel trade and furnace-tapping. When I had noticed the glare before I had dismissed it as a fair comment on most of the things that went on during the day. I was open to an explanation. "It is the glow of apocalypse. It means the world is going to end to-morrow."

He was clearly expecting from me some cry or hug of dependent affection that would dilute his bitterness. "Didn't you hear what I said, boy? It means the world is going to end to-morrow." "And a good job too," I said, with maximum savagery.

He led me back to the hole so that he could have half an hour of peace before supper.

2

Change Here For Strangeness

Short of having oneself weighed in diamonds and being frankly worshipped, I suppose the most one can hope for is to be able to live on differing levels of identity. Consciously, and getting the full flavour of the absurdities involved. Up to a point I've managed that. I am nowhere in the same class as those lads abducted from the homesteads of white pioneers and brought up as blood-brothers of the marauding tribe; nor Mowgli, step-brother to wolves, nor yet Tarzan pampered in his lodge of gibbons. I envy these characters. To look at humanity from across a wide margin of wild, tough alienation must be tonic.

In the shadow of these exemplars I offer my own experience humbly. I never made the wigwam and wampum belt. I never saw an ape or a wolf until the visit of Bostock and Wombwell's menagerie, an occasion made notable by the resident gorilla which almost choked the life out of an anti-Darwinian who was nosing around its cage looking for material to fling at the infidels in the Library and Institute.

I was abducted from my traditional mores by the death of a language. The tongue my people had been speaking ever since they started circulating half-truths about King Arthur collapsed on my cradle and the calamity can still take a large share of credit for the hard core of bemusement in my mind. I entered late boyhood in complete ignorance of the language my father spoke as his first choice if he wanted to say anything really significant. Whenever that happened I was usually the only person around, and this led to plenty of strain. It frustrated him and tired me. He once said that I was the only swine in the Celtic fringe that could not be seen for pearls.

The change of language sliced through a whole family. Of twelve children six kept possession of the old tongue. The bottom six

marched off to join Hereward the Wake, Dr Johnson and Wheeler
and Wolsey. The world was divided inside our very kitchen and
there was already enough going on in that kitchen. Congested
before, it became embarrassingly tight to afford stabling room for a
ruptured culture and a covey of noisy young refugees spinning like
schizophrenic tops as the ancient tongue went into its astonishing
skid.

When I was about ten there was an effort made in the primary
schools to win us back. The old language was already beleaguered
and stricken. If we had been on equal terms with the defenders we
would have shaken a pike and deployed our mutations with the
best of them. But having lost the advantage of growing up with the
thing ingrown we chose to remain wantonly outside the citadel. If
we were ever approached by patriots aboriginally gibbering, accus-
ing us of pouring salt into the wounded back of Llewellyn the Last,
we would rage back in our own brand of low-calibre English and
report them to the Agent for Indian Affairs. We learned mechan-
ically from the more brutal teachers a few autonomous phrases that
would not have taken us very far on a colloquial tour of the hinter-
land. *Y mae mam fy mamgi yn y nefoedd.* "My grandmother's mother
is in heaven." *Y mae bachgen yn yr afon.* "The boy is in the river".*Y
mae buwch yn y castell.* "The cow is in the castle." *Y mae Jacob tad Joseph.*
"Jacob is Joseph's father." And last, the darling phrase of every
militant politician who had fallen behind in his reading of the latest
pamphlets. *Rhwyn weld y bedd y dydd yn dod.* "Beyond the grave the
day is rising." Somewhere in these phrases is the germ of a musical
and little more.

Had I been allowed to follow my nose into a totally English social
medium my life would have had a smoother course but a flatter
quality. As it was we were thrust into a cosmos of moralizing and
mourning conducted totally in Welsh. We were surrounded by
people who seemed to have a mania for hustling the young on to
public stages as bullets in the fight against joy. I had a fairly mobile
face and a voice that carried. I learned, parrot fashion, a dozen or
so monologues in Welsh putting a dramatic knock on drink, lust
and social untidiness in general.

I became one of a troupe of lads on the didactic and propagandist
side of the Sunday School and Band of Hope. We found no difficulty
in learning the reams of Welsh and were no worse in our perform-
ance for not understanding a word of it. We worked out some

striking sets of gestures and reached a volume that bored through the thinner vestry walls. If ever debauchery was found smouldering in any part of the gulch we were rushed there like visiting firemen, and we dealt the bibbers and amorists a series of oratorical rabbit punches that left them dazed for days after our passing. We kept sin more sedulously on the hop than anything since the plagues of Moses. The peccant were startled to see mere children scourging thirst and incontinence as roundly and loudly as Elijah or Billy Sunday. If we had known what we were talking about we could never have done it because in the climate of that time we soaked in tolerance like air. Sometimes we were surrounded and molested by the more brazen of the dissolute, and this hurt us because we did not know exactly how we had angered these boys.

I wound up doing a sort of permanent turn with a boy called Goronwy Gadd. Goronwy who, at the peak of our partnership was about seven to my nine, had taken a severe social beating. His father was doing a long Wagnerian duet with the brewers, and his mother, a silent, inert woman, had less interest in clothing her young than a baboon. So Goronwy was puny and ragged, a gift of first-class grist to the Daughters of Temperance. They teamed him up with me but made no effort to feed and reclothe him. Goronwy was to be the resident skeleton in the cupboards of the lustful and intemperate. A local deacon who, when young and under the influence of rum, had committed some sort of folly against the main pole of the eisteddfod tent, wrote for us some of the most sombre dialogue since Timon of Athens.

Alongside Goronwy, I was as robust and personable as Diamond Jim. Goronwy, in the script, would ask me how I looked so well while he looked like something underneath the one stone that Dickens had left unturned. I would explain that my father was a drunkard, a man who had been carried home so often he got snobbish about walking. One Christmas Eve I had confronted him in the pub, thrust into his hand a huge sprig of holly and a minute replica of the natal crib I had made myself from a branch of the tree under which his mother was buried. He had admired the workmanship of the crib, then he turned it over to the landlord for a pint. I struck at him with the holly and he had followed me home whimpering. I told Goronwy where he could get holly and how best he could lure his father down to a level where he could feel the full effect.

Then Goronwy would say that not only was his father a hopeless drunkard but he was also after other women. I replied that I understood and gave him some figures to show the clear link between alcohol and extra-marital urges. My own father, the script said, had been an all-season adulterer. I had followed him on a Christmas Eve and had entered the room where he was in full cry with his mistress. In one hand I carried the customary holly and in the other a long empty stocking. This had puzzled the mistress and she had lain there a whole minute silent before ordering my father to seize me and thrust me up the chimney to meet Claus. But he had been touched and he followed me home whimpering. That was always the curtain line. The slow walk home and the penitential whimper. Goronwy, after about ten minutes of this, thanked me and said that I had put Christmas in a new light for him. Then he groped his way off the stage and as we walked up the aisle to our seats people peered at us to see if we were true.

The situation was full of richly stupefying possibilities and we emptied it. Three attendances each Sunday at the Welsh chapel were compulsory and if I demanded that my theology be funnelled to me in Bantu as a change from Welsh I was cuffed as a renegade. If ever I slipped from the conventicle betimes to head off an attack of rabies or migraine my father and a few of the brethren would be waiting for me on the pavement to throw me back in.

The morning service was bearable. We were fresh and strong and from the age of about four when we had got our eyes above the level of the seat in front we managed to do some fairly worthwhile ogling at the girls in the opposite gallery. There was nothing simple-witted or casual about this. Being totally out of touch with the gusher of words from the pulpit we put a lot of serious pagan venery into these exchanges of the eye.

This sort of nonsense was not possible during the evening service. Even an involuntary blink in the direction of the girls would be enough to have one gaffed by some bristling sidesman. This was the peak of our anguish of non-communication. Some of us reacted badly and plucked at the web of absurdity as the sermons wore on. Special platoons of hard-handed, dark-faced ushers were told to close in on us and still our tongues and bodies as we grew more restive. However bright the artificial light each service for us had the authentic note of nightfall. But my father insisted that we go. To behold the sight, if not to comprehend the sound, of a righteous man in a state of passion was bound to be instructive. He said that as a lad he had tramped ten miles to hear sermons of up to three hours. "And look at me," he said. We looked at him and had our thoughts.

The preachers of the period were all of the classic cut and any one of them who preached for less than ninety minutes at a stretch was considered to be something less than frank. The rhetoric from the start was hot, and the sermon would end in a spurt of howling shamanism, an ecstatic lycanthropic baying at the non-conformist moon. This was called *hwyl* or the spirit, except by anthropologists who just sat and took notes.

This last phase of convulsive exaltation was easy to take. It transcended language and creed. It would have had as exciting an appeal to an Eskimo as to a young Congregationalist, and indeed there were times when, flanked by the chillier type of sidesman, that chapel gallery felt a little like Baffin Bay. The *hwyl* was a miniature ballet of acted hopes and terrors, as precise as a bullfight in its rhythm of recession, advance, challenge, and triumph. While it lasted we leaned forward on the balcony of the gallery, drawn with a joyful helplessness into that vortex of tremendous, candent, world-slapping phrases of which we did not understand a single syllable.

3
Stay As Beat As You Are

I have always viewed as bold and outrageous the resolution of those who wish to change the lives of others. Revivalists, Utopians, morally concerned teachers have all, at some time or another, held me in thrall. But on the private ground floor of my mind I have never failed to see them as strange and elusive as yetis, and to be amazed, repelled.

Only once have I ventured out on this transformation antic, determined to change the fuse and direction of a life, to make a salvage-tool of my compassion. It was not an effort that had any effect on my own life. I was barely eleven at the time.

The role I chose was that of marriage counsellor, and if you are looking for a social impulse on which to break the teeth of pity that is the ticket, a mender of broken marriages.

In my part of Meadow Prospect was a lurching, improvident fellow called Percy Ferguson. If a preacher or deacon wanted an instance of a wholly lost and pointless life he would hint that we could do no better than to take a long, cold look at Percy.

Percy was not a conscious rebel. Once he had attended a session of the Moral Philosophy Class on the invitation of Gomer Gough, the class secretary, who had told Percy that, properly oriented, he could well become a victory missile of the Left. Percy listened for fifteen minutes to Nestor Harries, the class-tutor, and was led out of the room with cramp of the ear-drums and he took a swing at Gough as he was steered past the podium. He also invoked an old curse on Harries and all tutors.

On Saturday nights Percy was a leading figure in the drunken routs that swayed up and down the main street, putting in any oath or blow that seemed to be missing from the routine. In or out of beer,

in or out of English, he could be fluently obscene, and the Nightin-
gale League, a women's temperance outfit, claimed that they had
at least three charges on which Percy could be walled up. The idea
that Percy was coming at them from the shadows became one of the
best known psychological blockages of the zone among women.
But it was said that Percy, in the sex matter, was torpid and had
been seen breaking into a run only when about to fell some tavern
companion.

Percy was often in gaol. Most often this was for assault of the
generalized Saturday night sort, but occasionally he would break
into one of the less well guarded shops. His thefts did not cut deep:
they hardly amounted to more than a brief airing of the stock. Percy
attracted patrolling policemen like a magnet. One judge said that if
Percy had been known to make a more thoughtful effort to hang on
to his loot, he would have sent him to some thicker, grimmer gaol
than our own County Keep. In gaol Percy was a great reader of the
Bible and became one of the most eloquent cuckoos in the theologi-
cal nest. He could disconcert the pious by reciting passages from
the holy book that could be taken as providing a kind of sanction
for drink and lechery. For a week after each release he would move
about the village giving out a raking fire of Biblical questions. One
day he stopped me and asked me who were the three characters in
the Apocrypha whose Christian names began with F. I didn't know.
He told me.

He had a certain gift of repentance that brought him closely into
touch with us. During the Easter and Whitsun singing festivals he
would come and stand among the children in the chapel gallery.
He had big, inaccurate voice which he flung at the hymn like a
boulder. He always chose a spot of the gallery that was notably
hollow under foot and favoured resonance. When he struck a note
that offered him a safe saddle he stuck to it, and he would have
every loose floorboard in the place rattling back. He played havoc
with the final balance of the festivals, and more than once the
precentor sent agents to threaten Percy and tell him to cut it out
unless he wanted, one day, to go down before a penal pelting of
swung hymnals.

Percy never heard them. During these sessions he was at the heart
of an emotional storm. He would cry and sob and rescue names
from corners of his shattered past. We had heard that he had, some
years before, abandoned a wife and several children in an adjoining

valley. It was when we stared at Percy in these moods of penitential singing and weeping that we felt certain that he carried within himself the materials from which he could devise a new and tidier life.

As a Christmas approached we thought we saw our chance. The combined Chamber of Trade of Meadow Prospect and Birchtown were trying to think up some manoeuvre that would prevent the commerce of Meadow Prospect from slipping into a total swoon. It was first of all thought to rig up some kind of eighteenth-century coach that would roll into Meadow Prospect carrying a load of Sam Wellers who would proclaim a simple hedonism and try to talk the local dialecticians out of the anguished knots into which they had worked themselves over the years. But they found that the slopes of the road from Birchtown would put too much of a strain on a tall type of vehicle like a coach, and if the trip was made it was thought possible that stewards would have to retrace the route, collecting the Sam Wellers and reminding them of their scripts.

So the merchants settled for a rather squat, strong vehicle, half sleigh, half troika, to be pulled by a pair of spirited Welsh cobs and driven by some voter dressed as Santa Claus. The sleigh would be packed with gifts for the children of Meadow Prospect. There were many applicants for the job. The man chosen was well known for his sobriety, diligence and a way of belting sense and obedience into even the most skittish of Welsh cobs. He was also a man whose arms took on a slowness just this side of death when handing out gifts, so he would take so long distributing the packages it would emphasize the greatness of heart of the combined Chambers of Trade.

About a week before Christmas we approached my father and told him that this Santa Claus job would be just the thing to lure Percy Ferguson back to the lighted part of life. My father knew Percy quite well, had drunk with him, had worked with him for a short time on the ostling flank of a local mine, and had been the delegate appointed by the Institute to take gifts of cakes and thoughtful pamphlets to Percy when he was doing his various stretches in the County Keep. He regarded Percy as one of nature's bandits, too slow in argument, and too prone to erupt into violence. When we brought his attention to the great tracts of the Bible that Percy had learned in gaol my father said that these feats did not, intellectually, jack Percy to a much higher level than a smart budgerigar. "As for him being Santa Claus, he'd be a disaster. The horses that will be pulling that sleigh will be fresh from the hills and very wild. Percy as an ostler is on a par with Percy as a thinker: very poor. He will bring out the worst in these animals. He will cause them to kick holes in the sleigh and then they will do as much for Percy and those merchants who are promoting all this gaiety. What's more, if Percy were offered this job he would, long before Christmas, have handed the ponies over to the gypsies, sold the sleigh for kindling and done a great deal with a local fence for the great pile of gift packages."

We told my father how we had seen Percy sing in ecstasy at the singing festivals and weep as he got the full impact of remembered innocence and joy. My father was moved. He passed what we had said on to the one member of the Chamber of Trade who was in the market for extreme sentiment, and this man persuaded his colleagues that Percy was the man for the Santa Claus job. The merchant was impressed by the fact that a group of children should have shown such perceptive compassion. As a reward we were to be given our car-fares to Birchtown and allowed to drive back to Meadow Prospect with Percy in the sleigh. My father wanted to insure the lot of us lavishly and to turn the inevitable disaster into a possible doorway out of the slump. But the local insurance agents took one look at Percy, the sleigh and my father, closed ranks and just laughed.

We arrived in Birchtown at nine o'clock on Christmas morning. The programme was that at ten o'clock we should be high-stepping it into Meadow Prospect square, Percy roaring greetings and ourselves singing loudly enough to be heard above the noise of ringing hooves and the cheers of the children who would be lined up on the square waiting for their gifts.

There was no sign of Percy or the sleigh. The merchants were worried and wanted the police brought in and Percy stretched when they could find him. A messenger came up to say that since early in the morning Percy had been in the bar of a nearby drinking club where the steward, an impulsive lush, had ushered in Christmas by opening all his taps and, from what the messenger said, Percy had been waiting underneath each tap as it opened. The chairman of the Chamber of Trade went to the drinking club, banged on its front door with his cane and shouted upon the steward to open in the name of the law and seemliness, and to deliver Percy Ferguson to them under pain of seeing the licence revoked.

Percy came into view supported by two friends. He had on his

Santa Claus costume but it created no effect of merriment. The first man appointed to the job was much smaller than Percy, and no attempt had been made to shake out the hems and make the suit baggier. Even the beard looked tight on him and the only thing the short, white-fringed jacket and trousers did was to suggest that Percy was going to be brutal in some brighter, jollier but stiffer way than usual.

The sleigh, pulled by the team of Welsh cobs, was led out from the yard at the back of the drinking club into the square. A majority of the Chamber of Trade was for stripping Percy of his splendour on the spot and sending the gifts by post. I led the children in a plea for tolerance and to cut the argument short we helped to hoist Percy into the driver's seat. We watched him anxiously. What we could see of his face looked blanker than his beard. We pressed the long whip into his hand. All he did with it was to try and scratch his back. He scratched the back of the sleigh but it seemed to give him relief. The Welsh cobs were quite still — even torpid, and we heard the messenger say that Percy and the steward had been feeding them a bucket of beer every time they went out to the yard. The man who had been first appointed was in the crowd and making sounds intended to startle the cobs, bring out their natural fierceness and play hell with the sleigh. But the cobs were beyond caring.

We got into the sleigh. The chairman of the Chamber of Trade made a speech. He was a loud speaker and the empty square gave him plenty of resonance and echo. The dancing sounds brought a whiff of awareness to Percy and the cobs. They started to stamp and he cracked his whip at an angle that was clearly meant for the speaker.

The sleigh left the square slowly and it proceeded quite sedately through Birchtown. A few of the crowd followed us, among them the chairman of the Chamber of Trade, a magistrate, who kept putting up a certain number of the fingers of his right hand. These were the number of months that Percy could expect in the County Keep if any harm came to the sleigh and us.

Once out on the moorland between Birchtown and Meadow Prospect the tempo of the whole affair gave a jump. The cobs must have thought they were back on the mountains and a fresh, whistling wind brought out the charioteer in Percy. He started cracking his whip to a steady tattoo that finished off what little restraint the ponies had left. The ill-made road assumed the ruthless cant of a cliff. The ponies reached a rush of crazy speed. We lay on the floor of the sleigh, praying quite coherently that Percy and the cobs would choose the same moment to drop dead. That, we thought would reduce jerkiness to a minimum.

Then the sleigh stopped abruptly. We lifted ourselves out from under the gifts and peeped over the edge of the sleigh thinking we were now in Meadow Prospect square, and I gave the note for the song we were to sing in answer to the cheers of the waiting children.

There were no cheers, no children. We were still on the moorland. On our right a road climbed north over the hills. Percy was staring at a sign-post. On it was the name of the town where we had heard Percy had left his wife and children. His face was very sad. Our pity burst its buttons. We hummed one of the hymns we knew had coaxed tears from Percy in the past. They did so now and ruined the top part of his beard. I went close to him and whispered something to him about Christmas being the time of restitution, of healing. I had heard one of my teachers say it. It had moved me. It catapulted Percy.

Percy raised his hand to the sky and shouted that he was going home, home, home. Then he gave one of the most dramatic laughs I've ever heard. It astonished us and maddened the cobs. They started up the hillside road almost leaving their harness in the sleigh.

We reached Percy's native township. He drove the sleigh into a street of minute, dingy dark-grey houses. Percy got off and made for one of the doors. Four times between the middle of the road he stopped and looked back at us. His face seemed to have fallen back from his beard, shrunken by a cold, frightening cunning. Whatever heat or passion had fired him at the crossroads was out. I stood up in the sleigh and made a statement. I said that Christmas for Meadow Prospect would be complete if Percy were to return there with his wife, children and the fact of a life redeemed, all the ghosts of his ancient folly laid.

He knocked on one of the doors. A woman opened it. She had the look of one who, after years of fingering, has fought her way from beneath a classic load of social rubble. She looked at Percy and her face shuffled in a second from puzzled to appalled. Percy went in. We shouted on him to take some gifts but he did not turn back. He was out again in a few moments followed by the woman. I heard her ask "Who was it you were looking for?" "Percy Ferguson," he said. "He's been gone for years," she said.

Percy climbed up into the driving seat. I shouted to the woman that Percy had come back, but the sound of my voice could not be heard above the crack of Percy's whip and the hard surge of the cob's hooves. I saw the woman half-smile and her lips formed around the words "Thank God for that."

A quarter of a mile outside Meadow Prospect our gallop slackened and the sleigh stopped. Percy Ferguson pointed his whip at me. "Off the sleigh, you," he said. "Santa Clause has no place for troublemakers."

I got off. By the time I reached the town's square the gifts and the children were gone. When I was asked what I would like for next Christmas I said a muzzle for my mouth, a brake on my pity and a brick of indifference for the dissolute.

4
Explosion Point

During the whole of that first year in the County School I was fated to be heard by Mr Thurlow in some act of declamation. Mr Thurlow was a High Churchman, an austere traditionalist, the junior chemistry master at the school and his hearing was uncannily good if I were anywhere within a mile of him. I would go for weeks in a sullen silence, resting my cords after a gruelling series of shows in the vestry, then I would erupt. Usually, in the middle of some group of companions, I would stop and let rip with both fists at some sacred cow, some mossy old belief. After my expulsion from the Sunday School at the age of eleven and a half for arrant Pelagianism, Mr Thurlow heard me sounding off about the need for a jubilant anarchy. The Sunday School Superintendant, whose patience I had finally broken with my little dialectical ram, had been a man of some violence. He had expelled me the short way, down a flight of stairs. When I had got my limbs together and shaken one of them at the conventicle I slid round Pelagius and landed in a total doctrinal eclipse, and this I stated for the first time just as Mr Thurlow was passing.

That set the pattern for a small age. If ever I decided to launch a critical word at heaven or earth, Mr Thurlow would be there, nodding and listening. Once or twice it has occurred to me that some member of my group would catch a glimpse of Mr Thurlow from the corner of his eye and then goad me into utterance with a bit of subliminal muttering on some theme about which my spirit was tinder-quick. But I cannot think of any member of our troupe who was up to that level of craft. The simple fact was that I had a voice trained in the art of speaking from hilltop to hilltop and invariably bad luck in the public use of it. Also I had been made unduly vocal by an addiction from the age of seven to political meetings and demonstrations. I could imitate exactly the gestures and tones of about twenty local orators and usually did so with Mr Thurlow's ear right in my mouth.

What pantomime and prep school are to many children, demonstrations were to me. The conscience of the valley at that time was a kind of tocsin for all humanity. I could never hear a drum or see a banner without falling in. The banners were infinite. There were the big global things in which we demanded an end to hunger, bloodshed and yaws; there were the banners that pointed the hose at possible areas of fire. "Watch Chanak" or "Hands off Chepstow". There were demands for the release of imprisoned Radicals the world over and we had a long list. Some would be well known like Tom Mooney, Sacco, Vanzetti. Others might be local boys currently in the County Keep for railing at some or other aspect of the Establishment in public and in savage language. These demonstrations became a vast, universal act of communication. In one turn-out I saw a banner demanding the deportation of Joynson-Hicks, the then Home Secretary, followed by an utterly non-political clutch of marchers. These were pigeon-keepers blaming some quirk of government policy for the outbreak of some ravaging type of moult among their birds.

My presence at these events was noted by the organizers. On one occasion, to give greater poignancy to their demands, they asked me if I, together with another under-age insurrectionary, would like to carry the banner at the head of the procession. This was a banner with a brace of slogans, one in Welsh demanding that some brazen tycoon get lost, and another in English, pledging solidarity with the lads in some colliery two valleys away who had been on strike for two months and whose clashes with the police had the punctual stability of a fixture list. I was delighted. I grasped my pole and set off at a half-run that almost broke the arm of my partner, a slow hand with a pole and adverse to publicity. I rounded my first corner in fine style, a wheeling manoeuvre that threw the brass band off its beat. In the whole street there was only one person and he was staring at me. It was Mr Thurlow and his eyes said without reservation that he now thought I had finished the course.

From then on the chemistry laboratory at school in which Mr Thurlow taught became a battlefield. He taught us only during the afternoon session. By then his mood had lost whatever friendliness or serenity it might have had in the morning. There was some talk that he inhaled small amounts of ether as a stimulant and I certainly recall occasions when we came into the laboratory and found him bent over a bench laughing his hair off. We put it down to the fact that he had spent a whole morning thinking about the valley and putting up with the fantastic smell of the place in which he worked. But once he caught sight of me there was no more laughter. Whatever comic vision he got from the ether slipped through the floorboards as soon as I came into view. For him I was eternally rounding that corner with that banner.

First he would point at me and chemistry was forgotten. His lips would form around some of the black slogans he had heard from me bidding the weak be strong and the strong a bit more perceptive. Then he would shout: "There's the cheapjack, the mole, the tunneller. There's ..." And he would name one of the prominent left-wing gurus of the period whose axioms, he was convinced, I had now welded into a non-stop oratorio. Then he would pick up one of those iron tripods they put over bunsen-burners to boil things. The chase would begin. The thing became such a ritual we even hit on a pace acceptable to us both, enough to feed an exciting rage in him, enough to keep me just out of the range of the swinging tripod. When I hear people speak to-day of "enormous strides in chemistry" I still think of those grotesque marathons played out between myself and Mr Thurlow around and over those scuffed laboratory benches. They would end with his returning, gasping, to his private room, a tiny cubby-hole full of bottles. He would close the door, content, I hope, in a dark, safe silent world where his grey convictions rose solid as mountains in his unchallenged mind.

Just before I left the chemistry course for good Mr Thurlow and I looked at each other, for a moment, in a new and healing light. At the summer concert he had heard me sing a solo called 'I am dreaming of the mountains of my home,' a sweet lament which would move a camel. It tells of a rover who has been bitten and blistered half to death in some such oil outpost as Abadan. The rover is sick of Abadan and he wants to be buried in the mountains of his home where it is cool and the graveyard tranquil. The song made a deep impression on Mr Thurlow. He had never been to Abadan but he had been scalded several times by wrong mixtures in the laboratory and he had confessed to us that often, during country walks, he would go into graveyards and be impressed by the quietness and the absence of teaching. Our eyes met as I boomed the last note of the song, a major alto effect. We both wondered what exactly had fed the blight which had brought ruin to the earth between us.

I decided to make a last effort at creating a possible groundwork of peace, short of singing that song about the mountains every time he came into view. I asked who was the best boy in chemistry in the form. I had never got near enough to the subject to have any idea of how our ability in this field was mapped. I was told that one of my classmates, called Geary, was almost a genius, a boy who had his fingers just a hair's-breadth away from the philosopher's stone. I approached Geary. He was a stolid boy who, even at the age of thirteen, had his own little market garden and sold chicks and rabbits. He did not look like a genius but I had seen pictures of famous inventors on a set of cigarette cards and some of their faces had a moronic hang. At least three of them looked like Geary who himself had invented some new way of stimulating bucks or does.

I persuaded Geary to let me share the last experiment with him. He looked at me suspiciously as if he thought I was trying deviously to edge my way into the rabbit market. I told him that all I wanted was the experience of working in harness with a born chemist. He nodded and we set to work.

I watched him closely as he set a light to the burner and started assembling materials. I saw no hint of mastery in his style and I did not like the way he had of constantly putting questions to our neighbours on the bench. But I remembered Mr Thurlow telling us of a professor of his who had been so hamfisted that he had confined his research work to probing nature with the fatter type of retort. And there was also the possibility that Geary, while seeming to ask questions, might only have been testing our neighbour's knowledge. A born teacher as well as a born chemist. I worked alongside him with happiness and enthusiasm. Mr Thurlow looked at me warmly, as if hoping that I might still be weaned away from the aridities of language-study and won for the future as a maker of new synthetics.

Now and then I blew into the bunsen-burner to sharpen the flame for whatever climax Geary had up his sleeve. I started throwing in suggestions about what he should do to thicken the mixture that Geary was assembling in a flask. The complacency with which he took these suggestions, the children of a virgin ignorance, gave me a few moments of doubt, but Geary seemed to be growing in confidence and skill, and once or twice he walked away and came back with powders and jars that belonged to groups other than ours and saying in a voice that grew louder that we should not spoil the ship for a ha'porth of tar.

Then there came the point at which we must have put together the pincers of two enormous miscalculations. I blew into the burner and Geary added a spoonful of something to his cocktail. We were blown violently away from the bench. The flask, three pipettes and a tap vanished, never to be seen again. The porcelain of a sink was cracked right across. We shocked an asthma sufferer into a complete cure. Geary and I were both slightly concussed, with Geary looking very much the same as he had done before, but happier. As soon as I recovered I picked up one of the iron tripods and handed it to Mr Thurlow. We began, sadly and reluctantly, our very last canter. When, a vacation later, I entered the languages department, he double-locked the door so that I would never get out again.

The genius turned out later to have been not Geary, but a boy called Leary. The Welsh have an infirm grasp on their initial consonants and I had been misled.

5
Lapsed Policy

The central point of our indoctrination, as lads, was the draughts and chess room of the Institute. In this room gathered some of the most desperate theorists that ever dyed a concept black. Their disbelief had developed a fine, apocalyptic swing and they had us sold on the idea that man's athletic and cumulative idiocies would soon land the species in a punitive and paralysing stroke. If they ever played chess or draughts their games had never ended for neither side gave credence to the victors or defeat of the other. They existed in a sinister, doomed vacuity, and they could fill it at bewilderingly short notice with the craziest guffaws of laughter. We took up a total negation with the same fascinated delight that other children of our age gave to soccer or scouting. We learned when looking up at the stars at night to smile at the idea of a conscious design. If anyone said "God bless you" we sneezed. We had our staves up in perpetual defence to reject any advance by St Paul, Paley's Watch, Archbishop Wilberforce and Luther Reynolds, a local voter, who was hearing the gaiety of Sodom so loudly on the wind around Meadow Prospect he spent every other week-end queuing on Penarth pier for a place on or in the new whale.

Our group became a hub of infection inside the Sunday School. The superintendent and his aides fanned us with missionary posters when we came in to clear the air. They reckoned that we were able to take the gloss off three rows of pews with a few loaded precepts from Schopenhauer and Thomas Huxley, and regretted the passing of the simple age when the utterance of any impiety would have brought a rattle of penal bolts on the roof of the mocker.

The corner of the vestry in which our class functioned began to take on for the superintendent the alien look of a mosque or bordello. We swiftly wore out a belt of teachers. One of them got himself transferred from the theoretical front to the simple job of making cocoa in a large urn for Band of Hope socials. Another was demoted to take charge of a class of five-year-olds who, while touched with the prevailing cynicism, expressed it unclearly and without offensive force.

So the superintendent called in Arthur Moyle. Arthur was the chapel's theological trouble shooter, the firmest brush ever to be thrust up the ideological flues of the pagan. He was a bright-eyed, fast-talking young man of about twenty-six, an ex-student of a very thorough Bible school and incredibly quick in citing the scriptures, more fluent than Micah in the litany of damnation. The superintendent was sure that after three weeks of beating with the evangelical holly of Arthur we would be back in the misson-tent saying the good, strong word for redemption and grace and carrying burning links to the more materialistic shelves of the Institute.

We rode the gales well. When Arthur took over our class he was already past his apostolic best. Arthur had entered the insurance business at a time when the people were beginning to adopt a careless, even flippant, attitude towards death. They seemed to get as much enjoyment from seeing their policies lapse as in rosier days they would have derived from seeing flowers grow. He sold a lot of policies of the more modest penny or twopence a week sort. He had a way of invoking a portrait of doom poking its hand around the corner that had most of the suggestible voters signing up for full coverage. And many of Arthur's policies had a way of becoming payable just a few weeks after he had wheedled the first instalment out of the client. The company sent special investigators down to see if Arthur might be staging some monstrous swindle in conspiracy with his more demoralized clients, and on the Sunday following this visit Arthur waited in silence for at least a minute before telling us that profanity and lust were the things we had most carefully to look out for.

Arthur's career as a lover did not run much more smoothly. The father of the girl he was courting, an alert paranoid called Bartie Greenwell, kept bending over Arthur's affair and whispering warnings. Greenwell had read a number of ancient texts which denounced the double-life of monks and the perfidy of priests. He had Arthur tabbed as a monk and would stand outside the parlour in which Arthur was trying to organize his wooing, clearly speaking such axioms as: "The holier they seem the harder they strike."

The brother of Arthur's sweetheart was an uncouth jocose type of man who was not above thrusting his head into the parlour roaring on Arthur to drop his mask and get cracking on a programme of rampant, pre-marital license. A catalyst in the whole affair was the loss of Greenwell's rabbits. Greenwell was a substantial rabbit-keeper and the tenants of about twenty hutches had been wiped out as softly as a sigh in the baying saga of a cattle-plague which had denuded our hills of livestock. He would often join the uncouth voter at the door of the parlour and say: "It's the rabbits I'm on about, Moyle. Where was the justice of that? What harm had they ever done, Moyle?" This type of question, coming on top of the tensions that are bound to build up in an evangelist in love, tore lumps out of Arthur's fabric.

Sunday after Sunday we saw him fall apart. Two events supplied the final bombardment. The hard core of his insurance customers, after years of devotion to one of the bleaker branches of non conformity in which preacher and congregation spent long periods just staring at each other, moved on to some special mound of despair and decided to stay there.They opted clearly out of the conventional contracts of hope and amenity. They refused to use the municipal park and denounced even funerals as a superfluous frill. This meant that the kind of tidy, death-ridden thrift of which Arthur was the agent was out. They didn't go all the way with the Mennonites but they were up close. They marched together to Arthur's house and one after the other, speaking no word but "No," threw their insurance policies on to the tiny lawn that stood in front of Arthur's house. He came out saying "Yes, yes," but the tide of negation was in spate and he stood no chance. He gathered up the policies as if they were the leaves of some last terrible autumn and he wired head office to switch to something else.

At the same time his love affair had taken a grave jolt. One evening he had been in the Greenwell parlour with his sweetheart. The room was warm, Miss Greenwell complaisant and Arthur distracted and ready to shed virtue like a chafing slough. The tide of his desire had risen and touched the icy surface of his inhibitions. The air was full of hissing problems. Given peace Arthur might have fed himself to a devouring sensuality and an unstirring contentment. But at that moment Greenwell, who was feeding pennies into a gas meter just outside the parlour door, was reminded of the spectacle of Arthur's clients siding with death and gibing at the insurance company. Greenwell began to laugh and to tap out the rhythm of his joy on the meter, a cynical sound. When he heard it Arthur was in great distress. All the facets of his dilemma were around him like scythes. He started banging with his fists on the parlour's uncarpeted floor. Greenwell listened. Arthur added loud groans, groans of genuine perplexity, to the work he was doing with his fists. Greenwell was worried. He imagined that Arthur might now be working to some drastic programme of victory by seizure. He thought also of the dry rot that was given away free with every plank sold in Meadow Prospect and he was afraid that with a few more bangs Arthur might be slipping south to the sub-soil. So he broke into the parlour, lifted Arthur to his feet and bundled him out of the house. Arthur landed on the pavement in a state that set a new sweat and turmoil record in that part of the town.

The following Sunday he walked into the Sunday School. He was late. All the classes except ours had already begun. Arthur was slow in his movements, his face was ashen as if all the world's wisdom had burned out to some grey and terrible end inside his skull. Several of the teachers either started to smile or to hum one of our Christian marching songs to counteract the effect of apocalypse that Arthur had brought in with him. The superintendent nipped over from the advanced class and told Arthur to buck up, back out or go into the sub-vestry and brew himself a beaker of restoring cocoa.

Arthur took his seat among us. We leaned forward expectantly. We sensed all that had happened. We feasted upon his defeat. Our smiles were mordant cannibals moving in among his last frail defences. He stared at us all in turn. His huge, annotated Bible stayed unopened on the bench at his side. His lips had tightened into a shape that looked like the seal of a final compact with silence. His whole interior was whitening with the rising flags of surrender. His gravity began to disturb, then to chill us. I picked up the Bible, opened it at the page of Genesis on which we had last been doing some simple bits of exegesis. He pushed it away. He began to speak and his lips had to move several times around the words before they worked up the sound to send them out to us.

"You think it's easy, don't you?" he said.

"What's easy, Mr Moyle?"

"To teach, to believe?"

"Oh no. It's hard, Mr Moyle. You teach us now, Mr Moyle. We are where Moses killed the Egyptian, the foreman."

He shook his head.

"No," he said. "Moses can stay where he is, his hand still raised in the simple act of killing, still not knowing that he will pay for it with a forty-year walk to nowhere. And I'm going to stay here and you are going to teach me. You are going to tell me what you know, for a change."

He pointed at me.

"We'll start with you. You start to teach and you'll feel the bits coming unstuck."

We started. We laid before him the modest bundles of disbelief we had picked up at the Institute. We conveyed to him the essence of what our good, faithful ears had gleaned from the sages at the Institute: the elements of doubt in the story of the creation, parthenogenesis, in the tales of Jonah, the men in the furnace. We painted the vision of the universe as a pyrotechnic farce soon to blacken to its end in a mindless void.

When we stopped Arthur shuddered as if some last door had been burst open to admit some climactic wind. He stood up.

"You're right, you know," he said and went out.

He left Meadow Prospect three days later for the Abercrave area where he did well in his chosen business of insuring people. Only occasionally would the old earnestness fall upon him. Then he would pause in front of some nihilist or some sectary and he would just shake his head. And over the years he would approach the four of us in his Sunday School class who became teachers. He would look at us very penetratingly and just say "Well?" We never gave him an answer.

6

Reluctant Trouper

Most of us come through the years flanked by actors manqués who placate the virus by getting hold of us from time to time, plastering paint on our faces and pushing us into any strong light that happens to be handy.

My own Svengali was a teacher called Howie. Over the whole period of my youth he kept after me. I don't know exactly what kind of a dog Francis Thompson's Hound of Heaven was but if it was surer-footed than Howie I would be surprised. I am not sure what the Hound wanted of Thompson but what Howie required of me was very simple. He wanted me to act.

The relationship began in the Primary School. I was about ten. Howie was a graduate who had failed to get a Grammar School post. He was disgruntled, idle and apparently mad. He had a dark, dissolute face and his main tactic was to lean against a window ledge, looking at us from between his fingers, as if, for sanity's sake, he was rationing the sight of us. The school's curriculum was narrow and Howie, by the use of silent inertia, brought it to the point of vanishing. He was convinced that we were all perfectly able to write, spell and figure, but that we were all making a show of being misinformed to bring Howie a daily inch nearer his last seizure. At any show of idiocy he would shout: "Nature bleeds, but I didn't go to University to be a first-aid man. Wound it some more."

Howie was a Welsh nationalist. He swam like a duck around the tank of tears that is fixed firmly in any Celtic past. He wrote patriotic playlets. Howie had stared at me for a long time and he said I had the true truculent face of an embattled Celt, the sort of features that had looked down at the Saxons through the fogs of Snowdon, thickening them. I tried to explain to Howie that my scowl had nothing to do with my being Welsh or a bristling insurgent. I looked the way I did because I was in the first stages of nicotine poisoning, genuinely foxed in my attempts to find any hint of promise or logic in my environment, and subject to some terrible ventral upsets brought on by an unwise excess of lentils in the Meadow Prospect diet.

But I played along with Howie. The play cycle he had written had two wheels: anguish and insurrection, and I was the boy who did the major pedalling. My first appearance in each case was as a captive and in this Howie left nothing to the fancy. I would walk on to the stage bowed down by chains. These were very real chains and they slowed me down considerably. Most of the first act was taken up with me moving from the wings to the middle of the stage, clanking and enraged, to be told by some king or chieftain to get used to these trimmings because they were to be on me for life. I hated those chains. They had been left in the Memorial Hall by some escapologist with a leaking memory who forgot not only the essential details of trickery that would have him sailing out of boxes and sacks, but also left his equipment behind him. In the Memorial Hall he had had himself chained up and enclosed in a sealed barrel from which he proposed to make his escape in four minutes. The darkness must have put him off his stroke, or the chains were of too honest a brand. It took two coopers or hoopers to get him out.

The play on which Howie expended the most labour was one which showed St David founding his cathedral on the cliffs of Pembrokeshire where a couple of his shin bones can still be seen. There was some talk of my taking the part of the saint and I worked my face into a whole new set of patterns to be able to present a picture of gentle innocence. I thought that this might possibly mark the opening of a new phase of more tractable and nourishing relationships with my fellows, and I could shed that iron top-coat. But Howie was dubious. The sight of me fettered and revolted had become one of his drawing cards, and it seemed to pull a satisfying bristle of excitement over the dry skin of his psyche.

He enquired of a few local hagiologists as to whether St David had ever gone around in chains. They said no, all agreeing that David had been a fairly limber intriguer with a way of keeping on the right side of the gyves. Then Howie had the idea of casting me as the sullen landlord, a pagan bully, who takes pleasure in saying that he would much prefer to put David over the cliff than let him have the land required for building the cathedral. But Howie could see no way of having this landlord appear in chains. The whole point of the play was that from the beginning to the end where he is struck down by a miracle this landlord is a puissant and overbearing man.

At least that is how it was on the first night. The headmaster of the school was in the front row grinning delightedly from the moment I appeared. His name was Theophilus George; we called him Theo. He had long been convinced that I was the hub of various commotions in the morning assembly, gossiping and leading groups of choristers in simple parodies of the hymn such as "From Theo skill and science flow." He was very happy about the chains that Howie had managed to make my almost regular wear. More than once I had heard him say that my fetters should be beaten flat, fitted with buttons and made immovable. Whenever the situation in the play caused my shackles to be removed his feet would start tapping impatiently and he would remain depressed until I ran into the disaster and death that Howie's scripts had waiting for me like large terminals.

On the second night Theo moved the front row nearer to the stage so that he could have an even more satisfying headful of my plight. The boy playing the landowner was a powerful, inarticulate lad called Grafton James. His father was a pious, reactionary man who had taught Grafton to keep his thoughts small and recognizable. Grafton, for various reasons, hated me. He considered me a crafty dialectician, a glib infidel who enjoyed nothing more than standing on pavements scoffing at the Boys' Brigade of which Grafton was the Drum Major. He also felt that on the first night some of the blows I had aimed at him with my chains had been genuine. He was wrong. In those chains I never managed to work to a fixed programme.

From the start of the second public performance Grafton was clearly in a mood for mischief. When he spoke to St David it was in a harsh shout that would have won a bonus from Stilicho or Hengist and when he brought his cudgel down on David he meant business.

When I made my rush at Grafton there was a sincere malevolence in my approach. He side-stepped and Howie's script and I went hurtling off the stage at the same moment. I landed on Theo and we wound up with our heads well inside the same concussion. He had been leaning forward to catch the last nuances of my agony and a flying fetter had caught him at the back of the neck. When he came round he made a full statement in which he said that Grafton was blameless and that I had meant this landing as a climax of all the years of dark and steady work I had put in in the main hall removing the gloss of dignity from the morning service. He instructed Howie to weed me out from the actors' guild. I also had a chipped ankle which kept me out of the two-mile walking race for the under-twelves which Theo, who sincerely believed in bringing sadness and depletion back to the Celts, had organized for the following Whitsun.

That is why, my Welshness apart, I've always had a fancy for St David.

Water Boy

Ideally, if one is to write, one should be born on the banks of a great river, like the Mississippi, or fronting the ocean. That way the imagination has one wall down, open to every wind, and one can, at any moment, dicker with eternity.

In Meadow Prospect our relationship with water and eternity was enigmatic. Our rivers and streams had no majesty or depth. They reflected the sense of transience that overhung all our thoughts. Even if they maintained a regular course and refrained from fooling about in our kitchens in their hours of spate, we gave them the sort of respect afforded to the Ganges and the other sacred streams of the East.

Our part of Meadow Prospect was bisected by a brook. Its Welsh name was The Lost Brook. It emerged from the hillside, flowed raggedly for about two hundred yards, fell in an unimpressive waterfall into a dingle which was full of people who kept pigs and struck us as anti-social.

Beyond the avenue of sties and the ceaseless procession of bucket carriers, the brook joined our river, The Moody, which years before had lost the colour, smell and normal habits of water.

The brook, as an obstruction, did not bother us. We rarely passed over it. On its other side were the Anglican Church and the colliery manager's mansion, which gave the area an exotic and inaccessible look. Our own side of the brook was given over to an alternation of chapels and cottages, which maintained a competition in bareness which would not have disgraced an open steppe.

Our opportunities for bathing were slim and loaded with hazards. We sometimes took a dip in the less exposed reaches of The Moody, where the only unlimited facilities were for sepsis. These moments were rarely tranquil. Perhaps we knew that being up to one's hips in The Moody was carrying social realism too far.

Then there were women with sensitive eyes and a trigger-happy moral sense who would pause near the spot where we were splashing about, point at the unstable kerchiefs which were our bikinis, and screech at us to get clothed and away. And the police, who seemed at that period to hold a permanent brief against delight, lost no chance to get us as we fled. In retrospect they might have viewed a bathe in The Moody as making a formal application for the plague.

There seemed to be no great love of tap-water in the town. A strong seam of anarchism in the local thinking made all services laid on by the government suspect. And the municipal council of the period was regarded as a covey of loons incapable of providing a safe and sensible link between rainfall and the needs of the kitchen.

This mood of distrust was sharpened to bayonet point whenever anyone was ill. To give the patient the stuff that came from the tap was seen as treason, a filling of the body with substances that would depress nature's power to heal.

So if one of our neighbours should be dangerously unwell, word of it would be brought to the Sunday School of which we were members. The superintendent, a man who believed in unadulterated food and drink as ardently as he did in Holy Writ, would send us to obtain pure water for the invalid from a local spring called The Spout, a vigorous gusher loaded with mineral salts which came from the heart of the mountain by means of a roughly inserted pipe.

We carried the water down to the patient in bottles, and there was never any lack of lads to take part in this pilgrimage of grace. The Spout was a meeting place for young girls whose moral stays seemed to be looser than the ones they fitted around us in our part of the town.

We never saw the water cure anyone. The only ones who left their beds as a result of our service, seemed to do so only because they were terrified of seeing this procession of youths with puckish faces filing into their bedrooms with bottles of every shape and colour.

Besides there were several of our number so excited by the dryads who hung around the fountain, and blinded by the glint of early passion, they forgot to fill the bottles. Many patients had their state aggravated by having to wonder what they were supposed to do in their condition with an empty bottle.

All around us on the hillsides were small bodies of water that tempted us to dive and swim in the midsummer heat. Most of these ponds were reservoirs built by the pit-owners to lubricate their enterprises. When they were abandoned, they became the dumping place for such mining accessories as great lengths of wire rope. This was deadly stuff, with one hundred times the lethal force of weed.

Someone was always in trouble and we did more active under-water work than Cousteau, diving down and tearing apart the tendrils of wire that had one of our companions by the foot. Bathing in the reservoir was regarded by the coal-owners as high-class trespassing, because when not struggling with the wire we got some pleasure from it. So the police prowled incessantly around.

Haring away from them with your soaked clothes clutched to your breast had the single virtue of getting your blood back to normal circulation after a near miss on the bed of the reservoir. I can understand now why, even in those early days, the insurance companies looked at us coldly.

As ripe a menace as the reservoirs were the small ponds that formed in dingles on the mountain tops. These were shadowed and sinister places, flanked by trees of a grudging, crab-apple type. And around the banks, between the water and the trees, a morbid profusion of fox-gloves.

The water was cold beyond the line of duty. You could almost see the air above it recalling the shimmers that play on waters visited by major heat in other parts of the world. Dragonflies made their way from one end of the pond to the other, pausing now and then as if becoming more sure by the second that they had come to the wrong pond.

We suffered too. Cramp cut short so many conversations and movements our idiom was left with a permanent sense of shock and suspension. We spent as much time dragging each other out as we did in the reservoirs. Our hearts, on meeting the water, must have come quite often to within a half-beat of closure. Had we known then what we know now about digitalis we would have taken a quick chew at the fox-gloves before making the plunge.

Between these hazards we were driven to taking our chances in the waters of The Moody, risking Weil's disease, a trip to the Juvenile Court or blisters raised by the Calvinistic curse of our offended matrons.

Sitting The Monsoon Out

One of the worst things about education in Meadow Prospect was getting soaked to the skin so often in the course of getting to it. By the time we reached the top of the hill, unserved then by any bus, we were dripping. The wet boys were allowed to miss assembly and sit around in the large school cellar to dry off. We sat around on the high-piled cokes making a tremendous racket and looking like a witches' sabbath or a meeting in France in early 1793.

These sessions were a nightmare for our caretaker, Conway Flook. Conway was a dark, short, preoccupied man and no ordinary cleaner. He had won two prizes in a pre-war festival of poetry and song at Meadow Prospect for odes in traditional form. But he also submitted poems in a freer vein to our local paper, *The Meadow Prospect Messenger*. And these poems seemed to have drawn their symbols from cleaning and caretaking. We had kept cuttings of several of them, as:

> My years and days a crackling floor,
> My brooms have worn their bristles to the quick,
> The dirt of rage, regret and age cannot be
> vanquished more

and:

> The pipes that warm my heart are worn
> And cannot be renewed,
> The furnace, late to start, encumbered quite
> With slow inexorable ash.

We, who were students of the poetic impulse, were often fascinated by watching Conway walk about the school with some dark anger ripening in his face, realising that it might well evaporate into some act of high bardry. But he was a reserved man and he rarely uttered anything to us that could not have moved straight into the prose section of *The Meadow Prospect Messenger*. He was often taunted that the poet was his brother, also called Conway Flook, whom he kept permanently down in the cellar. We had put this theory to our friend, Ted Dolan, and Ted had earned the sharpest clip of the week while sitting on the cokes one morning drying himself. He had started rummaging among the coke and said, "Now then, Mr Flook, where's the captive singer, boy?"

The drying session was a good way of avoiding the morning assembly and the first lesson. All the boys who turned up were not genuine cases. There were some who came to school encased in so many layers of mackintosh they could have come by way of the sea and still stayed dry. But these lads envied the warm companionship they found around the furnace and they would often nip into school, peel off the top layer of waterproof clothes, and then stand under one of the many defective chutes in one of the school yard's quieter recesses.

But life had grown harder for the users of these chutes since Mr Rawlins had become the chief assistant and was showing off his zeal in every nook and cranny of the place. Mr Rawlins would hang about behind a window near some obvious fountain of rain water from the roof. He would wait to catch about three boys, dart out and drag them in. Then he would line them up outside the main hall, wait for the service to end and then ask the headmaster's permission to lead the culprits up to the stage where they would stand, dripping and looking daft, while Mr Rawlins gave a talk on the vices of guile and indirection.

One Tuesday morning the rain was special. There were at least eighteen boys down in the cellar when we got there. Wilf, Spencer and I, prefects, went around the group feeling trousers and stockings to make sure there was nobody dry enough to be upstairs. We climbed onto the cokes and made ourselves comfortable. Mr Rawlins opened the door suddenly and swept his eyes around to make sure that no one was smoking. But Conway had just done something to the furnace that had filled the place with smoke and we were barely able to be seen. This was a tactic often used by Conway to choke us and send us the more quickly back to our classrooms. But the average client of the cellar just sat there smiling at Conway, going dark brown and looking as complacent as a kipper. This got

Conway hopping. "If those poets of despair got a headful of drying boys as often as I do, they would have a cause to whine."

Conway was leaning on a broom in the corner, staring at life, cursing rain, keeping an eye on us and charging in to do a bit of noisy sweeping whenever some clumsy movement of our bodies caused a fall of coke into the clear space in front of the stove. Conway also managed as a rule to give a sly whang with the brush-head to some natural victim like Ted Dolan or Wynford Wilton, who spent two hours before school delivering newspapers and seemed to find some excuse for starting their school day down in the cellar even when they turned up at the gates as dry as a bone. Conway was wearing a black sou'wester on a slant and an oilskin given him by a tall, melancholy merchant seaman who had admired a poem about death written by Conway. The coat rubbed the ground as he moved about. In that costume he was about the most ominous-looking element in Meadow Prospect, and when he had his waterproof hat pulled down tight against hard rain and that oilskin gave out a sad, soft whisper on the ground, it was easy to imagine him as some kind of displaced, highly conscious beetle, a spokesman of all the creatures that led lives of fixed wonderment in Meadow. From his habit of marching majestically down into the cellar in this black rig and supporting himself on his broom, the boys often called him Pluto.

One of the troglodytes, a steady patron of the cellar called Royston Afflick, fished a soaked, ruined packet of cigarettes out of an inside pocket. His gesture was so tragic that Conway Flook chuckled appreciatively. "It's all right for you, Pluto," said Royston. "Very jocose, very snug, down here, driven mad by smoke and dust. And grown-up, not giving a damn. But us poor dabs, hounded. It's no joke."

Conway's face was moved to great and sudden pity. "Of course it isn't," he said. "There is no joke, not for you, not for me. As for being hounded, you are still in the lightweight class. Mr Rawlins is a relatively genial jester alongside some of the voters who are going to make it their job to unravel your happiness later on."

We all nodded. When Conway was in that prophetic vein he had an incomparable audience in us boys on the cokes. He laid aside his broom and prepared to hold forth. We urged him to do so, delighted with our sense of apprehension. "There is no joke," he said again. "And I'll tell you why."

He never did. Mr Rawlins entered with the force of massed artillery. "Upstairs! Upstairs!" he barked. "We are banishing darkness from the curriculum." We trailed out into the wet light.

The Heist

Crime in other areas may have an air of prosy practicality. It may get somewhere, connect, break through on solid professional ground. But in and around Meadow Prospect it always had a casual, nightmare touch. It never developed continuity, tradition.

We only once came near producing a genuine gunman. His name was Tal Treharne or, as he would have wished to be known if he had ever mastered the idiom of violence, Trigger Treharne. In his childhood he was quite pacific. His parents were quiet, restrained people. They joined every social welfare committee that was set up to provide people with milk, boots, foster-care or fruit juice, and as they made their way through life they left a wide wake of solicitude, milk, boots and so on behind them. Coming to think of it, all this committee work must have meant leaving Tal on his own a lot and feeling confused by the number of times his father and mother kept coming in and out of the door. But we did not think much of that aspect of the matter at the time. We would have said that until the time he was twelve Tal did not have one single illegal thought in his head.

When Mr Wyndham Watson, the new curate, came to Meadow Prospect he went to live with the Treharnes. Tal's parents were devoted to him and encouraged Mr Watson in his burning belief that he was going to stage a comeback for the Established Church that would make Wesley's bones groan.

We often heard Mr Watson in Tasso's coffee tavern trying to dent the unbelief of such free-thinkers as my brother Dan and his little group of philosophers, but the attitudes of these voters were as solidly wrought as the iron in Tasso's stove, and even though Mr Watson orated on a higher and hotter note than Tasso's tea urn, he usually left the shop looking as if he had just been speared in a Kraal brawl.

Mr Watson made a big hit with Tal, too. He was a prodigious reader of Westerns and could recite the names of the old gun-fighters, Earp, Materson, Bill Longley, Dallas Stoudenmire and the rest. He presented these men as simple moralists. Old Testament figures living and dying by a code of right and wrong to which we would do well to return.

We heard him advance these views to those boys in Tasso's and my brother Dan and the other materialists moved in a body up to the coffee urn and told Tasso to bring his steam to a full head. Mr Watson taught Tal the technique that had made Bill Hickock the fastest draw west of Natchez or somewhere. One night Tal demonstrated this draw to us as we sat around on the hillside above Meadow Prospect. We could not follow the details of the operation. It was done at top speed and looked somewhat like a man pulling his shoes on in an emergency. If Hickock's performance had been anything like that, he would not have survived his first duel without the help of cannon. Either that, or Hickock specialised in shooting people who were already lying flat on the floor.

Then, Mr Watson started a branch of the Boys' Brigade. There was at that time in Meadow Prospect a lot of militant pacifism and a cordial hatred of military and para-military bodies. Mr Watson wanted to wipe out these views. He was not discouraged by the ridicule aroused by the marching, the drumming, the pill-box hats of the brigade. In defiance he kept themmarching for abnormal periods, and a broad seam of fallen arches and calloused toes appeared among the young of Meadow Prospect. Tal was made a drum-major and Mr Watson gave him special practice, and Tal kept at it until his pill-box hat smouldered. My brother Dan had Mr Watson listed as the biggest knock since Hengest Horsa or Field Marshal Kitchener.

Then some over-pressure of affection developed between Mr Watson and Mrs Treharne. The sound of his rhetoric and the sensual flourishes of Tal as he jiggled and flung his drum-major's staff had softened the whalebone of her old inhibitions. She and the curate were caught in some rudimentary cuddle and the Bishop moved him farther north and advised him to switch from Zane Grey and Kipling back to St Augustine and Paley.

The Meadow Prospect Boys' Brigade fell apart, and we were not able to judge the size of the gap it left in Tal's life. Shortly after Mrs Treharne, tired of having Mr Treharne look at her for hours on end with a face full of quiet remonstrance, ran off with a huckster. Once again Tal looked thoughtful in a quiet sort of way. The huckster had Tal carry his bags full of hardware to the station on the first stage of their flight. The load almost tore Tal's arms out and the huckster was too busy stroking and embracing Mrs Treharne to give Tal a tip. This did not help.

When Tal was thirteen or so he saw a whole series of early gangster films with George Bancroft as the chief hoodlum. Dragnet, Paying the Penalty, and so on. Bancroft had a peculiar strut which involved a maximum protrusion of chest and buttocks. Tal fell in love with it. On Bancroft it looked good. Tal it made to look a cripple. He seemed eternally poised between leaving and arriving. When he came with us to the school clinic the doctor took one look at him and said, "This boy is pigeon-chested to within one hair's breadth of pecking and flying." And he prescribed a set of remedial exercises that nearly killed Tal.

When Tal was about sixteen and working in Tutt's Boot Shop he got his first gun, bought at ninth hand from Ludo Brisk, one of the darkest middlemen in the history of shady deals. He showed it to us one night as we sat on the Rocking Crag, a large rock and a favourite place for loafers in Meadow Prospect. He just showed us one half of the weapon and it looked a very feeble instrument to us and my brother Dan advised him to throw it in the river.

"Oh, no," he said. "I've got very definite things to do with this." He said the first item would be to hold up Tasso's and rifle the till at gunpoint. We told him we thought this was a terrible plan, and we reminded him of the many kindnesses we had received from Tasso, such as free toffee and cut-rate lemonade.

He said he had no ill-will towards Tasso, but he would plan his raid at a time that would allow him to throw a mortal scare into my brother Dan and those other pagans who had driven Mr Watson into early baldness and had probably deranged him as well, explaining his conduct with Tal's mother.

With the loot he would collect from his raid in Tasso's he would seek out and shoot the huckster who had dishonoured his mother. Then, if he had any bullets left, he would use one on Tutt the Boot Shop, who was driving Tal up the flag-pole with his barked demands for smoother salesmanship.

It was on a Tuesday night that Tal made his attempt on Tasso's. He stood in front of the till and tried to get his gun out. The pocket of his coat made a poor holster, and the gun was much too large for smooth manipulation. My brother Dan and his companions came to stand near him, interested to know at what he kept pulling.

Tasso leaned over the counter and asked Tal if he could measure him out two pence worth of his favourite brand of mint-lumps. Tal told Tasso to keep his mint lumps and tried to get his robbery under way. The gun came clear of his pocket and as it did so the gum and twine that Ludo Brisk had used to keep it in one piece must have broken loose. The gun disintegrated in Tal's hand and rolled in about six fragments into every corner of Tasso's shop.

My brother Dan and his friends, doctrinaire belivers in the theory that our main duty in life is to bolster the confidence of one's neighbours, collected the pieces and handed them back to Tal. While they were doing this Dan was trying to give Tal a summary of what Tolstoy and George Lansbury had said about violence and, on a more practical level, my brother Milo was telling Tal that if he wished to persist in larceny and gunmanship he should aim at large enterprises that could afford a loss, and stay away from small operators like Tasso who, at that period, was just managing to hang on. Tasso slipped Tal a bagful of mint-lumps, saying that a pleasurable sensation around the teeth had been known to do a world of good to the morals. Tal saved up for another gun, a better one. He showed it to us. We asked him about his future plans. He was secretive. He said he stayed firm on the private issue like Tutt the Boot Shop and the huckster, but he would allow his public swoops to be dictated by the twitches of opportunity.

He decided to rob an old man called Luther Waldron. Waldron was a recluse and was supposed to be a miser, vastly rich. He lived alone, occupying the downstairs part of his house only. The night on which Tal planned to winkle Waldron away from his coffers was a sultry summer night. For a whole hour before Tal approached the house Waldron had been trying to open his kitchen window to let some air in. He had opened the window and it had slipped shut again.

Waldron, tottering now in a half-doze, was lifting the window for the fourth time when Tal came down the garden path, his gun held rigidly in front of him. It went straight through the aperture that Waldron had just made. Waldron took hold of it with no sense of anomaly and used it to keep the window propped up. He said, "Thank you very much", and slouched back to rest. The whole operation had a feeling of aptness about it to which Tal could find no quick reply. So he went away.

It was at the beginning of the following summer that Tal made his last bid to sign on with Billy the Kid. His chosen victim was a green-grocer called Merlin Thurlow. Even among green-grocers you would not have found a man more melancholy than Thurlow. And that summer he was walking about on the grey rock-bottom of gloom. He had been threatened with distraint for turning his back on the rates question. His wife was hostile to the smell of vegetables, and the nearby river, after weeks of drought, had dried out and was giving out a smell like a sort of official shroud for Thurlow's view of life.

On the morning when Tal marched into Thurlow's shop, masked and armed, Thurlow's misery was at peak. He was unaided in the shop, shovelling potatoes from a sack into small bags for delivery. Trade had cheered up a little and people were once again taking a serious interest in chips. His wife was in a back room working a fan, cleaning the air and cursing Thurlow's trade.

The river was on top form discolouring the mountains and Thurlow's thoughts with its corrupt, indefeasible message. It had sent Thurlow's assistant into permanent duty in the Institute snooker-room, waiting for the rain to come and freshen Thurlow and the river bed. A rates-collector had just popped his head into Thurlow's shop for a quick look around as if trying to assess what Thurlow would be worth under the hammer.

When Tal stuck his gun into the leaning Thurlow and told him to stop fiddling with his potatoes and stand and deliver, Thurlow took this new visitation in his stride. All he said was, "What nonsense is this now?" and shoved a paper-carrier over Tal's gun. Then he said, "Help me get these potatoes bagged". There was a frozen edge of despair in Thurlow's tone that killed any wish to argue in Tal. He stowed away his gun and mask and stayed on as Thurlow's assistant for three weeks.

Then he went back to Tutt's Boot Shop. He is still there, a pensive, middle-aged man, and a slow worker with a shoe for sale. No more than twice a month does he give Tutt a look that speaks of some terrible decision. But he'll be all right. My brother Dan has got him reading Tolstoy again.

THE SEEDING TWENTIES

1
A Paling Darkness

When I was about eleven the nip of autumn was mitigated by a whiff of depravity from the senior reaches of the Band of Hope. We had been drafted into the chorus of a junior operetta of the Merry Widow type that involved a lot of fondling, waltzing and bussing. Deacons would appear briefly at the door of the vestry in which we did our rehearsing and say that the piece was nothing more than propaganda for bland sensuality. And indeed we warmed to this story of Viennese smooching, and as the melodies and words slipped into our blood-stream you could hear the laces of our moral stays go snapping to ruin. After rehearsals couples were seen drifting up into the lane behind the vestry, and even the glow-worms dipped their hindlights in respect. Deacons flashing cautionary torches into the shadows used up a battery a night, and the more vigorous amorists were told to stay away from the backwall of the vestry, which was in a subsidence zone and liable to crumble under any major pressure.

Alongside this a small wave of thieving was detected. A store of the Woolworth sort had opened in the town. The long, open counters with their rich variety of gew-gaws threw a splash of heat on minds made frigid by an Arctic economy. Bands of youths massed together and ravaged the counters as brutally as Jutes. Five shopgirls had dangerous hysteria at the sight of so much movement among goods having so little effect on the till. The manager wired off to Woolworth to ask him what he had done wrong. Two shopgirls were seen playing a kind of demented chime on two tills that had not taken a penny between them. The moralists linked this with the Viennese revels in the vestry, and the defenders of honesty and chastity raced up to their watch-tower, the trumpets of warning to their lips. A local historian suggested that the whole action was the last part of a deal initiated by the Phoenicians, a race that had once done a fair amount of loose bartering around Siluria.

Solutions were offered. The operetta group was told to tackle no theme earlier in time than the Book of Genesis. The multiple store manager was told to narrow his doors, higher his counter, make his counter-display more forbidding, his goods less portable and arm his shopgirls.

Into this situation walked Seithenyn Hamer, a Meadow Prospect boy who had spent twenty years as one of the most zealous missionaries to leave these shores and confuse the people of Africa and Asia. Hamer had covered more territory than a migrant stork and had had some narrow escapes. He had been nearly eaten by some Andaman Islanders who had only abandoned Hamer, a lean and craggy man, when some likelier looking dish turned up. An acolyte on whom Hamer had been trying out the theory that ground rhinoceros horn had a powerful aphrodisiac effect had turned on Hamer when crazed with depletion and tried to float him over the Victoria Falls. A rubber planter had had him speared for spreading dissension among his workers. Hamer had some phobic objection to rubber and had slowed down the production of the stuff as drastically as leaf rust.

Hamer's meetings in Meadow Prospect's Central Hall were very successful. He brought the evangelical urge of the place back to red heat. I have often wondered about the sight and sound of such a man on Peter the Hermit, who poured the scalding urges of mediaeval Christendom over an already fluid situation in the Middle East. I would say that Mendel would have had Hamer and the Hermit tabbed as springing from the same pod. Hamer convinced his audiences that a few major doses of missionary zeal would put paid not only to the mild outbreaks of venery in the Band of Hope, and the raiding tribesmen who had stripped the multiple store to the bare boards, but also to the fits of rancour and spite that were currently making our local industries hop and grimace.

One of Hamer's loudest devotees was Miss Jocasta Gee, a sweet looking but stern woman, a daughter of our Sunday School superintendent, Mr Moelwyn Gee, a builder, a stony, Mosaic figure who liked nothing better than to stand above some young offender, not saying a word and just touching the youth's brow with his beard. I list among the ten most truly odd sensations of my life the routine of being silently brushed by Gee. One wondered about what sort of moral carpet one was going to land on, and that was about the only sort of thought possible in the context. Having a lot of short pupils, as one is bound to have in a Celtic Sunday School, it meant that Gee needed a long beard. It was very long and never failed to make contact.

Hamer had written a whole fleet of sketches showing the hazards and beauties of missionary work. My teacher in Standard 4, Kingsley Pugh, was very fond of Miss Gee and he rushed forward at her suggestions that he should produce these sketches. Pugh whipped me in as a leading actor. He was convinced that these playlets projected by child performers would purge the zone of lust, looting and class-enmity. He saw them as being of particular benefit to me. As my body shook with the first tremors of adolescence, my mood had become sullen and caustic. Absurdity and deprivation were beginning to rub raw on my flesh. I was beginning to get the full, minatory measure of an environment that was going to leave me as pitted as a Swiss cheese. My head was beginning to fill up with a gravel of hard, philosophic thoughts. I was found shaking my head wearily at the Sunday School teacher. I was seen pencilling crude Marxist footnotes on the bases of missionary placards, and I was even suspected of being one of a group that had removed a ladder from the front of a house on which Moelwyn Gee had been doing some job of roofing. Pugh meant to put an end to all that.

He launched me on a world canter that still has me feeling that I have the continents beneath me like so many fields. Miss Gee made our costumes in her front-room. It was a small room and she had a wild hand with the needle, and all the costumes looked flimsy and the same. It didn't much matter because in each sketch I was a fractious young peasant with his ear in the mouth of some local Mao Tse-tung and dead against missionaries. During my fittings Mr Gee always sat in the room, rolling his beard between his hands, trying to put me right on doctrine and pumping me about my part in that ladder job.

Hamer's plots had been hammered into a rigid pattern by the starkness of his own experiences. In one sketch I would be a Malayan boy whose father is about to be sold up for back taxes. The missionary comes along and I come out with some Buddhist runes and challenge his Yahveh to change the world's tax policy. The missionary kneels and asks that I have patience, that salvation will come. It does not come, but the tax man does and my father is carted off to gaol and the house dispossessed. I run into the jungle, furious. I am bitten by a snake. The missionary sucks out the venom. I see a new truth and persuade the local radicals to turn their banners into Zenana League sashes and go back to their paddy fields.

And so on, around the globe. I became one of the most significant puffs in the wind of change. The pattern never varied. Insolence, resentment, rage, flight, then trouble and salvation. As an African I get it from a rhino and the missionary slaps some healing leaf on my groin. Cured of the goring and my ignorance I pacify the tribe. As an Arab boy I get it from a camel bite and the missionary cleans the wound with a simple pen-knife and the camel follows us around trying to express a change of heart as nearly as a camel can. The muttering Bedouin take one look at my transfigured face and shut up. As a Pueblo Indian maltreated by a tourist whose change he has tried to shorten in a trinket booth, my fractures are set and I am persuaded to give my trinkets away free with inscriptions on them about the need for a brisker trend in ecumenical affairs. I also break up a meeting in praise of the ancient Sun Gods and persuade the people to come down from those holes in the cliff, and build a chapel on the flat, on land donated by the tourist with whose change I had interfered. He was very keen to get the chapel built quickly so that if he found his change beginning to float again he would know where to come for me.

My performances were watched with interest and widening eyes by the left-wing in Meadow Prospect. They denounced me as the most inscrutable acre in the whole blurred map of our political disputes and social malaise. They dredged up some voters in the Library and Institute, ex-soldiers, ex-sailors or just liars in training, who came along to me with stories of missionaries who had been little more than dupes and tools in the hands of ruthless salesmen and they even suggested that I had seen Hamer himself draining away, by means of shady practices, what little light remained on the Dark Continent. With regard to those offensive rhinos, camels, tourists, and so on, that had run me down, I could take their word for it that Hamer had probably been behind them, guiding and directing them as weapons in the endless war to blunt the hopes of the progressives. But I reacted torpidly to these tales. Pugh, Miss Gee and Hamer had me in thrall. My brain had been washed so clean it lit up my part of Meadow Prospect. If I saw anybody in the town who looked as if he might turn out to be a muttering tribesman, I would go up to him and urge him to cut it out and come to terms with decent loyalties and honest labour. The last bid of the radicals to break my run as Hamer's puppet was to present me with a 'put-and-take,' a simple gambling device which was spreading a fever of gaming through the gulch, that had the older prophets stepping forth, shaking the ash from their togas and pointing to the moon, which at that season was red and baleful. I threw the 'put-and-take' into the river with a gesture that was later copied by Fiorello LaGuardia.

What was more I sincerely wanted to help Pugh. If, I argued, my work in the missionary sketches would help him in his courtship with Miss Gee he might become so happy in marriage that he would forget about his ambition to make me the major valve in Meadow Prospect drama.

Miss Gee accepted him. A large tea was given in the vestry as a way of thanking all who had helped in producing Hamer's cycle of improving playlets. Mr Moelwyn Gee was there and at the sight of so much tea and innocent gluttony even his dogmatic furies took a rest and did little more than let out a quiet bark as a token gesture of alertness.

Pugh bought Miss Gee an expensive engagement ring. The wedding was to take place the following spring, and the couple would leave the church under a human arch made up of people from the YMCA gymnastic group, who had been on loan to Pugh to simulate mutinous tribesmen hellbent on scaling forts and missions.

The marriage never came off. A week after the ring was handed over Miss Gee left Meadow Prospect with Hamer. They made their way to Waziristan, where they operated a mission in the hills from a rough hutment. Hamer's luck stayed bad. Almost at once the tribes, under that Fakir, started to simmer. If Pugh could have saved enough money and collected his thoughts sufficiently after that concussion he got from the ring deal, that is where he would have sent me, just to see whether drama and life ever do really meet.

2
Scalping Party

You will have heard of Eifion Pawley but not under that name. He has just been given an acting award. For twenty years he did good work in horror films, underlining the darker phases of fright with his thin, sensitive, cautious face. At the moment when the newly assembled monster or revived mummy appears, out from some corner comes Eifion, his skin paler than lilies with panic and his eyes inches ahead of his nose. Consternation shading into terror, that was his speciality. And now, with the taste in fun becoming more sombre, Eifion has emerged as a sort of comedian. You may have seen his last film. In it Eifion is a scientist on the mad side and a choral conductor. He fosters a breed of musical mutant with two heads which will double the volume of the singing while cutting down on transport costs.

I know something of how his gift began to flower. It was the summer of 1927. In Meadow Prospect, currency had practically ceased to run, and our sense of social exile was so acute that we were surprised to learn, through such oracles as the papers and the wireless, that there were still organs of government in London looking grave and going through the movements.

So we lost no chance of saving a few coppers. When a young neighbour of ours, Colenso Barnes, got himself a second-hand hair clipper with a view to training himself for professional status, we went instantly to him for a free clip. He operated his practice in the lane behind his house. He sat his client down on a thick, squarish armchair, which upset all those who had seen films with a Sing Sing background.

Colenso was no stylist. He offered one type of crop only. It was called 'the kronje' after some otherwise forgotten Boer leader, who had worn his hair forbiddingly close to the skull. Colenso would start at the brow and keep mowing until he met cloth at the back.

In rush periods he would often remove the whole eyebrow from the lower type of forehead. Colenso's 'kronje-cut' became a mark of boldness and virility and in our part of Meadow Prospect we padded about like renegade monks, keeping our heads low as if wishing to flaunt our defiant bareness.

The one customer Colenso would have liked to get into his chair was Eifion Pawley. Eifion had deep, wavy, silken hair that was the pride of his parents. They were poor but fancied a bit of elegance, and Eifion's mop was about the only bit of panache left to them. They had made it clear to Eifion that if he ever allowed himself to get within business reach of Colenso's clipper they would shoot Colenso and disinherit Eifion. Eifion took to darting away in panic every time he saw Colenso with the clipper in his hand and Colenso, in turn, got into a way of staring at Eifion's sheeny crown with a kind of sad lust.

The barer we became the more devoted were Eifion's parents to preserving the integrity of their son's hair. They would not even allow him to be gently trimmed by the town's one surviving professional barber. His blue-black waves started bushing out at back and sides like a monstrous wig. Sewell the Sotto offered him the lead in a juvenile cantata he had written about Samson and Delilah, but Eifion's parents pulled him out of the cast as soon as they had seen the end of the script. When Eifion walked among us he looked like the last unscathed palm tree on a fire-gutted atoll.

One afternoon I sat on the hillside near Colenso. He was fingering his clipper and staring at Eifion, who had started up the slope towards us and had turned tail back to the valley bed at the sight of Colenso. "He doesn't know it," said Colenso, "but that head of his is ripening towards me like a fruit ripens towards the sun."

At about this time Eifion and Colenso fell in love. Between the two girls concerned there was an odd link. Both their fathers were among the darker tassels on the depressed fringe of Meadow Prospect's religious life. Their names were Selwyn Sutro and Meurig Minns, and they were the saddest-faced men ever seen off the stage. They often marched up and down the High Street with sandwich boards bearing minatory slogans, of which the lightest and merriest was: "When sin freezes the hub, the wheel will stop."

Colenso was in love with Muriel, the daughter of Minns. Both Minns and Sutro regarded Colenso as a pest, a man whose fleshliness and flippancy should have brought a daily bolt upon his head.

His activities as a barber, his curriculum of shearing, which had the place looking like a prison yard, they regarded as natural and acceptable, something which would have a special part to play in helping the world on to its imminent burning. Minns had told Muriel that if he were to catch her with Colenso he would give a pre-arranged signal to his friend, Sutro, and they would fix Colenso between their rushing sandwich boards hard and flat. He had invited her to watch them practise this routine with the boards and she had warned Colenso to lie low.

Sutro was much less violent towards Eifion, who was too young to be considered as a serious sexual menace. There was also a hint of the desperately penitential about Eifion's uncut hair that made an appeal to Sutro, who believed that with doom about an hour off and winding itself up to strike, haircuts were an impertinence. All the same Eifion had come hurtling down the lane behind Sutro's home more than once with Sutro close behind him, travelling fast and threatening to fell him if he caught him hanging around his daughter again.

The situation brought Eifion and Colenso much closer. They were sitting one evening on the small stone bridge over the brook at the top of Meadow Prospect, and talking about the curious jest that made it possible on one earth for genuine affection to exist alongside such loveless and dangerous loons as Sutro and Minns.

Then Eifion's face started to darken. "I'm not getting anywhere with Sheila," he said. "I think she's cooling towards me. Sutro's reading out tracts to Sheila or putting something in her porridge. She's cooling."

"It's your hair," said Colenso. "With that great dome of hair you're carrying about there's an effeminate look about you. More than effeminate. Since that traveller came around buying hair at so much the hank, there's not a woman in Meadow who could come within an ounce of the amount you are wearing. Allow me to shorten you by about three inches all round and you could approach Sheila with a much bolder air. What's more, since Sheila's had that short bob, she told me herself, she feels lost when you cuddle. When she brings her face close to yours she feels as if she's vanishing into a thicket. And that's no good for love or anything else. So just come down to my chair and let me have a go."

It took Colenso a week to break down Eifion's resistance. And one Sunday afternoon, when Eifion's parents were off a whole day's evangelical jaunt up the valley, Eifion took his place shyly and with several articulate reservations in Colenso's chair.

It was just after tea-time and the Sunday evening's quiet had a jagged edge. We were uneasy as we grouped ourselves around Eifion, and there was a note of doom in Colenso's gesture as he unfurled a clean cloth to drape around Eifion's shoulders. The sunlight was grey and autumn went trembling up and down the lane. We knew why we were disquieted. The night before Colenso had been brooding about Muriel Minns, had drunk two gills of cider at 'The Celt Betrayed,' and then gone to stand outside the back door of Meurig Minns, roaring with passion and demanding an end to puritans and perverts. Minns had come to a window and thrown things at Colenso, but his aim had been bad and Colenso nimble. Under cover of the confusion Muriel had crept out to be with Colenso. Minns had discovered them and throughout the whole morning of the Sabbath morrow, Meadow had been full of long statements by Sutro and Minns that they would act on behalf of God against Colenso before the sun was down.

Colenso was pale as he limbered up his clipper finger. His eyes kept moving to the top and the bottom of the lane. We were sorry about this. We would have been glad if he could have concentrated all his vision and care on Eifion, who was getting jumpier by the minute. Just one word of encouragement and he would have been out from under Colenso's cloth and headed for home. "Now don't forget what you said, Col, a nice quiet, moderate trim. Just enough to make me look virile. Just the merest touch of the clipper for goodness sake. None of the shearing that gives such a squat, squalid look to the rest of these boys."

"Don't worry, Eif," we all said. "Colenso's touch will be like a feather. You won't feel the metal. Just enough off back and sides to bring your face into view. You're too much in the shadow now. A girl like Sheila wants to gaze, not peer."

Then there was a buzz of sound from the bottom of the lane. Minns and Sutro came into view followed by a small cloud of voters wishing to pass the time before evening chapel or discouraged from going up the hillside by the threat of rain. There were also a few, standing close to Sutro and Minns, hostile to Colenso and his slashing, aquiline syle, who were egging the two prophets on to unreasonable acts.

Sutro and Minns were wearing the long, heavy type of sandwich-board they favoured for statements of the blacker sort, and their progress up the lane was slow and deliberate. Of the two, Minns was a little faster and we watched the print on his board grow clearer. It was a mixture of eye-test and siege.

"Stand your ground, Colenso," we said. "Just carry on with your trimming of Eifion and stare them down."

Colenso got to work with the clipper. He started its journey, not resting lightly on the surface of the hair as he had promised, but hard and sternly on the skin of Eifion's neck. Eifion was too absorbed to notice, and leaned nervously forward in the chair as if wishing to hasten the climax of the encounter. Colenso did not once look down at Eifion's head. The clipper mounted to Eifion's crown and followed straight on down to the brow, leaving a broad, staring furrow. I tried to pull Colenso's sleeve and remind him of his vow to use only a light touch with Eifion. When I drew his attention to what he had done he grunted an apology and started his clipper again. He traversed exactly the same route. When I told him that he might as well spread the ruin now that he had made such a good start, he gave me a look so blank I could see that all this thoughts were on Muriel and Minns.

Sutro and Minns came to stand on either side of the chair. They were beating their boards to a rhythm similar to that which usually acts as a prelude to butchery in jungle films. Sutro looked hard at Eifion's head, now looking like that of a badger with the bald furrow white and plain as a Spanish road through the high hedges of blue-black hair.

Sutro nodded his approval of the way that Eifion looked and muttered that it was just the thing to keep the young modest. He even shook Eifion by the hand and told him he could call around to see his daughter any time he felt the impulse. Colenso was now beginning to smile, thinking that Minns and Sutro had entered into some new urbane phase, and that the danger to him had passed. He made a few gay gestures with his clipper and pointing at Eifion's head said: "Now I'll shear this boy's bush into a better proportion." And he pursed his lips to suggest that he was going to put a subtlety into this job of which we grossly shorn elements would never have thought him capable.

He was an inch away from Eifion's head when Sutro and Minns charged. If Colenso at that moment had not stepped back to get Eifion's hair into better perspective and his thoughts about it into a more artistic froth, he would have finished up as part of the punctuation in the slogans of Minns and Sutro. The sandwich boards and the heads of their wearers met with a bang that left Sutro and Minns a little concussed. They swayed about in a brief coma and seemed glad to be there. It took them several seconds to set off at a jog in pursuit of Colenso, who was already at the top of the lane.

By now Eifion realised what Colenso had done to his hair. He was running his finger up and down the furrow as if it were an old wound. We tried to comfort him.

"It's dramatic, Eifion. It's like looking up Cheddar Gorge or something." "It's fine, boy. You remember Magwa, that chief we saw in that film about the Mohicans. You are him, boy. Spitting image."

Eifion got up from his chair. "I've got to go home for my cap," he said in the voice that was later to become famous in the cinema when Eifion was asking the monster not to choke him there and then. "And if my father doesn't get nosey about it I'll keep it on for the next six months."

We followed Eifion home. He was making an extreme effort to cover the whole furrow with his arms. He looked deformed.

Near his home we were met by one of his neighbours, a man of a roguish and free-thinking type. He was chuckling to himself. Even after he had seem Eifion's hair-cut he kept on chuckling. And after our experiences with Sutro and Minns we felt that neither side in the conflict of faith and detachment inspired us with much confidence.

"I've just seen your father," he told Eifion.

"He's up the valley," said Eifion, "whorshipping."

"No he's not. The preacher this morning was a scorcher. He had your father sitting so hard against the chapel seat he could feel the varnish burning his leg. He was taken dizzy and he got up and said he was on the verge of some vision that would clear up practically every doubt now kennelled and snarling in our midst. He was taken out and given three glasses of hot mint-extract, your mother thinking that all this talk indicated some crucial bout of wind. He landed home an hour ago. He's in the kitchen looking as if he's been hit by a meteor."

We went up the gully that flanked Eifion's house. The dark had come and the kitchen curtains had been drawn. Through a chink we saw Eifion's father staring at the fire, looking just as he had been described. He had his hand raised as if ready to block the oncoming of some too brilliant light. Eifion took one look and said he'd rather flee there and then and take a chance on Patagonia. We opened the door and pushed him in. He still had his arm curved defensively over his head.

We learned later that Eifion's father, at that very instant, was about to make his revelation: that God had now finished his first total survey and was going to put some definite mark on those he considered mainly responsible for our long-distance distemper. Then in came Eifion, crouched, his face hidden. The howl his father gave sent Eifion's arm leaping towards the latch and the furrow came into full view.

For the next hour Sutro, Minns, Colenso, Eifion and his father went orbiting around Meadow Prospect, joined vaguely now and then by people who believed in pursuit on any terms as a salutary ethic. Then a weary wisdom fell upon the whole contingent and they trooped pacifically into Tasso's Coffee Tavern, where they all had an iced cordial apiece from Tasso, who was against haste and fanaticism.

After his fourth delighted sip at the cordial, Minns turned to Colenso and said that Colenso was now free to do as he wished. What Minns meant was that he had now given up the moral ghost and was inviting Colenso to do as he pleased with his daughter. But Colenso took it the wrong way and sheared off the rest of Eifion's hair that very evening.

3

It Figures

It is likely that even without any human relationships my journey
upwards from the abacus would have run into a few air-pockets.
But with Mr Glenn's assistance I was able to achieve a classic
alienation. It was a unique regression. By the time we had finished
determining the height of the pole up which we were driving each
other, I had slipped further back in mathematical time than those
first Egyptian grain-garnerers and pyramid builders who stumbled
into the first low arcades of arithmetic and geometry.

Mr Glenn was the man who kept bowling sums at me for most of
the time in the County School, and consciously I never left the
pavilion.

He had been a pioneer member of the Royal Flying Corps in the
First World War. The legend was that he had early become inter-
ested in the problem of correlating the movement of the propeller
with the projection of bullets from the machine gun. An absorption
in this question had caused him to become more and more absent-
minded. On his last flight he took off without adjusting his straps
and as he left the ground his brows and chin were down in the most
intense meditation. About fifty yards off the ground the solution
struck him. In his elation he looped the loop and fell out. He landed
on soft ground but the concussion destroyed the memory of the
climactic equation that would have put us ahead of Fokker, and
made Mr Glenn's moods from then on some of the least predictable
things in Europe.

His mind wore a mantle of ragged disenchantment. In his days as
a flyer he had known an exhilarating pride of which a classroom of
boys was the black, polar opposite. In the middle of his lessons he
would adopt a defensive technique of total withdrawal. He would
stop in the middle of a word, put his head on one side and go off
into a kind of trance. It was not an inactive, healing silence. Some-

times his lips would twitch into a sort of smile as if some memory of flight and the infliction of swift, heroic death were hovering like a flare over his shadowed mind. Some splinter of despair worked its way towards the surface of his mind and when he came to, the first boy his eye landed on was for it. It was almost always me. If Mr Glenn had returned from his recession into a world of darkness and if I, in that world, had been the only lantern, his eyes would not have been swifter to pick me out.

I tried evasive action. I moved about that classroom with the fluency of Houdini. I tried the sides, the front, the back. I would hide behind classmates, try altering my expression with grimaces that put two or three of my features permanently out of plumb. Mr Glenn's eyes would get to me like tracker dogs. When his rage exploded it did not send its shrapnel over a wide area. He kept every particle of it for me. He had an ebony ruler and his target was the top of my head. The modern taboo against head-hitting for fear of brain injury had not, at that time, surfaced, and could my pate have been the very centre piece of Mr Glenn's whole ravaged life, he could not have pummelled it more ruthlessly. And as he hammered and my mind rushed around in search of the flap that would open on to a coma, he would keep shouting "So you are the boy who thinks the rules of geometry are too overt and banal to need explanation." I could not remember ever having propounded any such doctrine but Mr Glenn had me tabbed as its author. After a year of that, mathematics had achieved in my thoughts exactly the place of sex in the mind of Cotton Mather or drink in that of Billy Sunday.

A nascent talent for mental arithmetic, an almost electronic power to shed light on those sums that crop up on shopping trips, that had shown itself in the primary school, limped off out of sight, its both feet broken beyond repair. Nothing has dimmed the bloom of that initial outrage. If, as it well might, a wild hatred of mathematics will one day qualify as a damnable heresy, I will walk gently and proudly as Latimer to the stake.

The years that followed were a kind of slow bullfight, myself the wary calf and Mr Glenn the clumsy torero. In his classes I sat in a corner in a sort of muttering exile, looking at him only when he dumped his endless problems of weight, price and space to one side and recalled his days of violence, telling us how, aloft, he had by lightning bits of trigonometry landed his bomb-loads on pin-points of German fortification and marshalling yard. Mr Glenn was a man who had genuinely enjoyed seeing things burst apart. Whenever we hinted with our eyes or a borrowed aphorism that there might be a strong case for leaving humans and things in one piece, he would lapse into his fissure of pale, mute wrath. He would look at us all in a way just two degrees less accusing than death, then he would jump two years in the course, chalk a problem on the board intractable enough to shame even the sharpest reckoner in the group.

In his relations with me he kept me more or less incommunicado. He would sometimes throw a question at me which would expose the pre-Nilotic innocence of my notion of areas and volumes, and he would add that I was a fair enough specimen of a mind cretinised by a garrulous and irresponsible social environment, a monster begotten of some terrible coupling between hymns and pamphlets. He suggested that I might be operating as a resident oath-giver for some kind of anti-scientific Mau-Mau. The least I could do was to play up to him by looking as monstrous and conspiratorial as I could and every time he passed, when I chanced to be talking with a member of the junior school, suggest by gestures that I was binding the child to some compact that would one day have us holding the head of Pythagoras under the waters of the Taff to a count of eighty.

At the end of Form V, I thought I was taking formal leave of Mr Glenn. I handed in to him the text-books which for years had darkened my life into a night of contagion. He said not a word to me. I said not a word to him. It might have been the last red corpuscle saying a last goodbye to the last bacillus, and Mr Glenn's eyes made it quite plain which of the duo I was.

But there was to be an epilogue. A new headmaster shook the curriculum in ways that provided a redoubt on which the battle could stammer into a final phase. The new man was porous to any suggestion that came from Mr Glenn. The fact that he had taken no part in the war put him on the defensive in the presence of Mr Glenn, who was a hero and said so.

The Sixth Form, when I entered it, was exploding with change. Brilliant blazers and grotesque caps of green and yellow with tassels were introduced for prefects. A system of competitive Houses was established, offensive to a generation nourished on Robert Owen and Thoreau. Hierarchy and social fission were as popular with us as yaws. Worse, two periods of mathematics each week were made compulsory for all members of the Arts Sixth. This was a definite manoeuvre by Mr Glenn to counter the markedly left-wing flavour of the teaching done in the Literature and History Departments. Even in the Languages section where I was quartered we had a teacher who could induce in us a sort of subversive sympathy with irregular verbs. "The maimed and limping under-dogs of philological caprice."

I decided to do something about the mathematics. A pliable doctor whose garden I weeded certified that the act of multiplication or the sight of a diagram brought me out in a state of urticaria, that Mr Glenn, in short, was the mother nettle of practically every rash I would ever suffer from. When the Head and Mr Glenn seemed to be on the point of denouncing the certificate as the work of Van Meegeren and the doctor as the son of Cagliostro, I said flatly that since I regarded mathematics as a more brutal and squalid caper than war I would object conscientiously to it and simply stay away. I was given permission to occupy a solitary place in a corner of the main hall and pursue some private study. Now and then Mr Glenn would look in, glare at me and hint that he was in touch with the spirit of Kitchener and would, without question, fix me.

He nearly did. When I got into the Second Year Sixth I had no wish to be a prefect. That cap with the tassels frightened me. My neighbours, lovers of sombre headgear if ever there were such, would elbow me into a leper's solitude if I flashed that thing at them. And I had loathed since childhood the function of supervising and the fact of being supervised. Shepherding the young made me feel a sheep. When I was in sight of the Headmaster I started up a racketing smoker's cough and a curvature that would have caused the collar of any decent vicar to spin right round.

But I became a prefect. When Mr Glenn pinned the green badge in my lapel I could see that he was setting me up for something. When the anarchists in the Welfare Hall first saw me in that tasselled tile of authority they shook my hand in commiseration, then laid the cap on a table and carried out some act of exorcism.

The tensions found their blow-hole. It was prize-giving day at which the prefects were to be ushers, dignified in mien and tidily clothed in sub-fusc. Mr Glenn had been appointed to a Headmastership in an adjoining valley and to mark the occasion he had been invited to serve as guest-speaker. He made it plain what his theme was going to be; the moral duty that had come to him on his countless dawn-patrols "when all the world was clean and only courage counts." We had heard it often. We had had fragments of it stuffed into the corners of every theorem in the business.

I did not feel I could go. Local orators bruised my mastoid bone. Mr Glenn drew it out and threw it to dogs. More, I could not be tidily dressed. Things had never been so rugged on the clothing front. Credit facilities had hardened to a point where a person in need of a suit had to go in blasting. Animals whose trapped pelts might have covered us had gone north to the mountains or taken to the sea. And my father had a friend who had received a commandment in dreams to use his needle in making suits for the penurious. I was his first sitter. The material was flimsy, his needlework sketchy and his measuring tape dim. If you can imagine a three-piece sarong that was it. When I first walked down the street in it I felt I was putting myself in jeopardy and the chapels in peril. My first appearance in school in this rig might have caused laughter. It did not. I looked too sinister to be clownish, a small pre-Brechtian figure of apocalypse.

The morning after the prize-giving Mr Glenn came gunning for me. I was sitting in the back of a class of linguists discussing French poetry and trying to figure what Rimbaud would have made of that suit I was wearing. Mr Glenn's wrath landed on the desk like the tablets of the Lord. It was hard to tell one whizzing word from the next but most of the syllables added up to a charge of betrayal. I had, according to Mr Glenn, talked five or six friends in the body of prefects into staying away from the prize-giving. I had not done so but they were in flight from the peacock in that twilit time. They had no wish to turn up at the chapel in which the ceremony was held to move up and down the aisles as the shabbiest ebb in usherdom.

I was on the point of making some profound and dusty apology. I must have arranged my features into the wrong pattern. Mr Glenn started tugging at my prefect's badge. The pin stayed firm. He tugged harder. Mr Glenn went flying backwards. In his hand was the prefect's badge. With it was the lapel and some other part of my jacket.

Five of us were broken as prefects. At the end of that lunch hour we were to file past the school war memorial and hand in our tasselled caps to Mr Glenn. We walked up the steep little hill that led to the school gates. We walked up it slowly, the fancy caps in our hands. A phalanx of young sympathisers marched alongside whistling or humming the Dead March from Saul. I had not changed my maimed jacket. I carried it like a wound.

I was the last to hand in my cap. As Mr Glenn extended his hand to take it he stared at my coat. He turned pale. The absurdity of waste and anguish in our long relationship showed naked. He pushed the cap back into my hand and walked swiftly into the school. I and my degraded companions walked to a clump of trees behind the school where one could smoke and be sonorously reflective.

That evening a package was delivered to my house. It was from Mr Glenn. It was a jacket of thornproof tweed, delicately and deliciously green and soft, and as near as anything to a perfect fit.

I wore it the next day to school. I did not say a word to Mr Glenn, but I made a great play of sitting in the very front row of his special mathematics class. The theme was trigonometry. The immediate matter was the advantage of knowing if you were about to hurl yourself from a lighthouse or a cliff, where exactly you would land. Mr Glenn spoke passionately and directly to me, and for a few seconds he and I felt that the whole wound of our joint being was being measured for the unguent. Within fifteen minutes of the lesson's end my head was rocking in a black tedium. I had taken the dive from either lighthouse or cliff and I knew where I had landed, on rock.

That evening I delivered the jacket back to Mr Glenn. He was not there. His wife opened the door. "He'll understand," I said, and pelted back into the shadow of my cosy perversity.

4

I Am Trying To Tell You

Have I ever given you anything for your birthday?" my father asked me. "No," I said, without hesitation or bitterness. I was ten and gift bearing had never been much to the fore in our family. I was used to the silence we had grown accustomed to drawing over all those occasions that set up bouts of fondness or weeping in most families.

My father looked at me in a way which I am sure he thought significant and moving. I was disturbed. The old soil of indifference had been hard but secure underfoot. I liked it better in that state. I had seen my father before, trying to reverse the levers of some fixed family convention and he had invariably wound up in some kind of noose with plenty of company inside the rope helping him to take the strain.

"Well," he said, "I am going to make up for it this year, don't worry. We are shuffling past each other to the grave like hooded monks and it's got to stop."

My birthday was three weeks off. I was convinced that my father had forgotten all about it. But one afternoon I came into the kitchen and found him reading a weekly magazine which told you how to become a mechanic at home. I was surprised to see him reading this periodical. I thought of my father's record as a mechanic, inside and outside the home. His way with tools had always been untidy. If ever he fiddled with a tap he kept the lifeboat stocked, and the neighbours for a block around were alerted to watch out for falling washers.

The next day I saw my father in deep conversation with Randolph Shand. Randolph lodged in a house two doors down and considered himself an enginer of genius, although his job, like my father's, was concerned with the upkeep and guidance of the pit ponies underground. He suffered as much as my father from the violence and ingratitude of the ponies, and it was often when Randolph and my father were standing in the penumbra of a cloud of oat dust, dreaming of a better lit and horseless state, that the ponies laid their hooves on them with the greatest vigour.

Randolph had often caused a lot of displeasure at the Debating Society in the Institute by standing up and saying that the slow crawl through trial, error, agitation and self-discipline of the common folk to full conscience and dignity was a lot of nonsense and would be quickly out-dated by new sources of mechanical power "One turbine will be worth a million prophets," he had said. "Everybody born henceforth with a dreamer's brow should be given the bottle with one hand and an oil can with the other."

We could see that Randolph was delighted with what my father had to say. He would grin and nod and keep pointing at something in the Home Mechanic which my father held open in front of them.

Then they began carrying small bins of equipment into the shed behind the house. We were forbidden by my father to go anywhere near the shed. From the look on his face we could feel no less than that he must be assembling a powerful bomb with which, using Randolph as a kind of fuse, he would strike a blow for lacerated ostlers everywhere. We stayed away from the shed with pleasure and even asked my father if he would mind shifting the shed a little farther away from the house.

Then a long pole appeared and a great length of wire which my father placed in such a way as to serve as a perfect trap for anyone wishing to use the retreat at the top of the garden. My father assured us that he had nothing against people using the retreat and merely warned us to tread warily.

The man in whose house Randolph Shand lived, Leo Powell, became disturbed. Leo was a twitchy, bitter man, driven almost to mania by his failure to get promoted and by his hatred of the radical dissent he sniffed on the social wind around him. He was the only Celt in Meadow Prospect who was still telling the Normans not to worry and shaking Edward the First by his mailed hand. He regarded Randolph with his phobia about gadgets and his mutterings about horses as insane, and my father he brushed off as a blasphemous nuisance. At the first sight of the pole and the wire he reported to our policeman, Ophie Pinfold, a muffled thinker and an ex-heavy-weight fighter, that Randolph and my father had their eye on and were preparing the material of some social coup.

Leo reminded Ophie of Grindel Mathews, a scientist, who at that period was in the Breconshire mountains working on a death ray. My father, said Leo, was probably an out-station for Mathews and in no time, when my father threw the switch, the voters would be frozen solid in their tracks. Mathews and my father, said Leo, had now come together for some astounding bit of international anarchy. Any day now deadly rays would be bouncing off the Chief Constable's helmet.

As my father and his group were preparing to plant the pole Ophie came up and laid his hand heavily on my father's shoulder. My father dropped his end of the pole.

"What's this now, Ophie?" he asked.

"Leo was telling me of some voter who is up in Brecon devising a ray that will stun or freeze or otherwise harden people."

"Why bring in a ray for that? It's going on all the time."

"Mathews calls this thing a death ray," said Ophie.

"That's right," said Leo Powell. "The death ray. Grindel Mathews's death ray. A thing of terror, and with an article like that about why worry about the rates?"

"Leo says he knows people who've been coming down from Mid-Wales and passing through Breconshire suddenly finding a strange, stiff feeling in their muscles. They've passed through the place where Mathews is at work and he's flashed this apparatus at them." Ophie touched the pole with his foot. "I don't like the look of this pole either. Leo thinks that with all this wood and wire, and padding about so furtive with Shand you might be on the same track as Mathews, and that the people you miss with the ray you'll get with the pole."

"Look, Ophie, that helmet is over your brain like a shop blind. Roll it up, boy. Tell me, Ophie, I know that you and the other constables keep your talk pretty narrow, deciding on who next to wheel off to the County Keep and so on, but surely you must have heard of Marconi."

We could see a thumb in Ophie's mind flicking through a card index of Italian caterers in the area. He shook his head. The index stopped at Luigi Mantovani who kept a teashop in Birchtown.

"This Marconi," said my father, "invented wireless. Most of us, Ophie, get by without thought, pity, wealth or point. Now we are going to be without wires as well. My friend, Randolph Shand, and I have built a wireless set in the shed there. It's a birthday gift for my youngest boy. You've heard of birthdays. Tomorrow they are opening the new broadcasting station at Cardiff. The Bishop of Llandaff is consecrating something or other and they are broadcasting the ceremony. We are going to launch the set with this item."

Half a dozen helpers fixed the pole upright. My father patted it and leaned against it to make his last statement of the afternoon. Ophie Pinfold and Leo Powell watched us like Sioux scouts.

"Tomorrow," he said, "at two-thirty sharp, the switches will be thrown. We'll be tuning in to the world tomorrow afternoon. The Celts will step out of the small parlour they have been renting since the time of Cadmon. The cult of tears and runes which has been our way of life will be swapped at last for a brisk diet of gossip and laughter from the great world outside. And Ophie, you'd better come too. You could do with being exposed, if only for a minute or two and in a shed, to the Bishop of Llandaff."

We started assembling at noon the next day. As we fled into the shed my father stood at the door nodding gravely in greeting at us all as if, all over the world, we could hear the rustle of a page being turned. If we did not, he was there to rustle for us.

The Bishop's broadcast was due to begin at half-past two. By two the shed was full and there was some groaning from a far, congested corner as Ophie Pinfold, in civilian clothes, squeezed himself in. We grouped ourselves solidly around the crystal set that Randolph Shand had designed. Oliver Powell, Leo's son, was with us. Leo spent most of his time guarding Oliver, a slow thinker, from the contamination of our company. His father had locked him in the kitchen to prevent his attending the ceremony in the shed, but we had helped Oliver out of a window. He was staring at the crystal set with drop-mouthed adoration as if expecting the thing itself to break into dance or flame.

"Let's have the music, Walter," said Melville Selley, who was sitting on a sack of potatoes, surplus to our needs and left alone for long, too long, and now as musty and soft and old as life itself.

"Where's Shand?" asked someone else.

"Randolph is making a final, last minute adjustment to the head phones," said my father. "He is at work at this moment down in our kitchen because you voters would not give him enough elbow room up here. He is at work with his screw-driver bringing the head-phones to a tip of sensitiveness that will fetch in the breathing of the unsatisfied dead if we get fed up with the Bishop."

"Here's Shand now," said Waldo Treharne, who was standing at the door of the shed looking most unbelieving, and keeping the door cautiously off the latch in case something went wrong.

A way was cleared for Randolph. He was ushered in by my father as if Randolph were a surgeon and the case dark. Randolph was carrying the head-phones on one arm. Whether Randolph had made or bought the phones, I never knew but they had a bigger superstructure than any I had ever seen. A rhino could have slipped them on without tightness. When Randolph put them on, his head seemed to be vanishing into a gaol. When the superstructure rested on the top of his head the phones were on his shoulders, giving Randolph a look more of being decorated than effective.

We all watched Randolph tensely. He looked crushed and trapped beneath all that metal. He leaned over the set and switched on. We all pressed forward to listen.

My father waved us back. "This thing is delicate," he said. "Even warm breath could play hell with it."

Waldo Treharne closed the door of the shed and the lessening of light brought our senses to tiptoe.

"When the sound starts," said my father, "when the bishop starts coming through, the phones will be passed around, gently and in a disciplined way. Don't let excitement at Marconi's miracle trap you into snatching at these very sensitive contraptions."

"Turn it up there a bit, Shand," said Melville Selley, who thought that Randolph was selfishly keeping the sound to himself.

Randolph's lips were moving without speech. Some thought he was reporting something he had heard, but to others it just looked like an invocation and it did not seem to be getting very far. Our surrounding heads were now almost touching Randolph, and the sense of being enclosed and overwatched made Randolph's eyes stand out more than usual. Between his face, the phones and the coils he looked like something brand-new to this earth.

"Stand back there," said my father. "The sound that should be coming into the phones may be getting sucked into your heads."

My father was stung by some bit of irony from a far corner into giving the set a peremptory thump. Then vaguely and very far away a voice was heard. Randolph slapped a phone back to an ear and my father slapped an ear to Randolph. My father, convinced that he had got into touch with the right wire when he gave that first thump, slapped the set again.

The voice came nearer. We all looked at each other, blinked respectfully at Randolph, nodded our heads and said, "The Bishop from Llandaff. He's here in the shed."

As the voice increased in power and definition we noted that it had a quality of bellow about it and a lot of its sentences seemed frankly to end on a note of witless rage. This caused several of us to wonder, although we had never heard a bishop before, but my father stamped on the thought.

"It's the bishop telling off the laggards who are drifting away from the faith. It's a few more angry clerics we want if the Church isn't to go down for the count. Scalding rage, not soft benediction. That's the ticket. Think of Thomas a'Becket."

"Who?" asked Ophie Pinfold. There had been a Thomas Becket in the area some years before, an anarchist so baldly subversive that the chief Constable had ordered a double thickness of wig to keep his own confidence in our tribal taboos. Becket had been put in gaol two or three times and Ophie thought my father might be putting in a word for him under cover of this seemingly harmless demonstration of home crafts.

"Thomas a'Becket," said my father. "And the Bishop of Llandaff is following his example. The Bishop is doing very well. He has swung right into the hwyl, the fervent peroration. No dawdling doubts with the Bishop. This is a new revival, fully dentured and utterly dour. The Established Church is doing all right. I'll say that, fragmented non-conformist as I am. The Bishop's doing fine."

He was. By now he sounded rather more than half mad. And to all except Randolph Shand, my father and a few bemused voters sitting near Melville Selley and those potatoes it was clear that the voice was not coming from Randolph's set or earphones. It was coming from outside and it was heading rapidly for the shed.

The door of the shed was flung open, sending some of the listeners cannoning into Randolph who waved them back in a frenzy. We all looked around. Leo Powell stood by the door, his arms upraised in wrath. His was the voice that had been drifting up from Llandaff. He hurled himself through the little audience and siezed Oliver by the shoulder and threw him against the table on which the set stood. As the table rocked and fell Randolph's body was galvanised. From the headphones came a shriek of atmospheric sound and the single word "God" spoken clearly and solemnly as a heavy bell by the Bishop; who must by now have been in the very last phase of his dedication. The set burst apart as it hit the ground and a new sort of silence altogether formed around the apparatus on Randolph's head.

No one reproached Leo as he led Oliver back home. We walked up to Randolph and shook him gravely by the hand. The last to congratulate him was Ophie Pinfold who said he saw nothing to fear from the new medium. My father was the last to leave the shed, just behind me. He took a long, sad look at the wreckage and was reminded of something. He touched my shoulder.

"Many happy returns," he said.

5

So They Came And They Took Him Away

Smedley gave the smallest pennyworth in the history of the potato, and if you complained he would tell you to read up what had happened to Ireland in the 1840s and to thank your lucky stars.

My father and his friends, on the grass patch by the old steam fan, often spoke of Smedley and his sombre approach to the chip trade. "It is clear," said my father, "that he is nursing some grudge big enough to break both his arms."

One night my father and Waldo Treharne had a chat with Smedley during a lull in the frying. They said that they wished to give him formal welcome to Meadow Prospect, but added that they were convinced that such brooding secretiveness as his was bound to affect the quality of his materials, even the fish. "Don't forget, Mr. Smedley, if you have a trouble, confide in us. Don't be a man on your own. If you've fled into the chip traffic to escape a broken heart as other voters flee into the Legion, you'll find Meadow Prospect the sort of place that can slap your gonads back into life and keep them singing. Not a licentious place, mark you, but working always to a steady beat."

That same night Naboth Kinsey was asked to take his gramophone and records and play them on the small vacant lot behind Smedley's shop. Naboth functioned as a kind of mechanical Orpheus in that part of Meadow Prospect, and in any part of the town where my father and his friends felt a need to give comfort to the sick, the old, the lonely and disabled, Naboth would carry his great horned gramophone. We would follow close behind him with the records and the low table on which the gramophone would rest during the recital. Behind us came my father pondering the nature

of the audience we were likely to have and arranging the pro-
gramme.

About thirty yards from Smedley's shop was a row of tiny houses.
It was called simply The Slope, and in one's mental vision it was
always heading sharply uphill as if trying to get away. In these
places lived a high proportion of people who seemed to have
withdrawn utterly from the life of Meadow Prospect. A crust of
neglect had formed over people and dwellings, and one could not
speak of them without feeling that men, women and tottering stones
were heading for some quiet and sinister fusion. In the third house
of The Slope lived a young widow of striking loveliness and blackly
inconsolable. It was to this place, these people, that Naboth Kinsey
now turned the horn of his gramophone.

Naboth was given his head in choosing the programme. He
brought out his incomparable collection of Caruso records. Early
spring was stirring among the hills, and every shout of rebirth and
loving reassertion found an echo in the great brazen beauty of
Enrico. I was in Smedley's shop when he first heard 'Celeste Aida.'
His head shot up from its sad business over the pans and his hand
with it, sending a spray of hot fat around the shop that caused some
of the clients to think that Smedley's misanthropy had now entered
a new and actionable phase. They told him to take it easy unless he
wanted them around the corner, mixing it.

Then they saw the radiant emotion on his face, brilliant behind
the very heavy texture of his black moustache. For minutes Smedley
stood over the range, transfixed, translated to a plane as far above
chips as a plane can get. We reported this reaction to my father and
Naboth, and they laid in a stock of gramophone needles big enough
to bore through the walls of any Troy of rejections that Smedley
might have built up in his heart.

The young widow in the third house of The Slope came out, sat
on her step, smiled quietly at the great triumphant flight of Enrico's
voice, sniffed the sunlight as if tasting a new fruit and began to peel
the layers of inward darkness that death had left inside her to be
called for later. That evening she came down to Smedley's for the
first time, was greeted by him with a passionate stare and a mon-
umental twopennyworth salted personally by Smedley.

It was the 'Niun mi tema' death cry of Otello that caused the
highest rapture in Smedley. When he first heard this, and Naboth
had had the gramophone brought up to the back window of the

shop so that he would lose nothing of the flavour, he dropped a bag of chips to the floor and turned fourteen clients out of the shop, and cried a little as he stood over the bubbling pan. Our Assistant Sanitary Inspector, Simon Wimpey, said that this was a clear breach of the Pure Food Regulations and told Smedley either to toughen his fibres or cry away from the chips.

It was on a Friday night, after Naboth had put on a whole flight of superb tenor laments by Caruso, that Randolph Shand walked into the shop.

"He's dead," said Randolph.

"Who's dead?" asked my father.

"Him. The singer, the lovely singer. Caruso, with Naboth out there, coming from the horn. He died in America. Hit the loudest note of his life, they say, and the breath never came back."

Smedley's jaw dropped almost into the chip fat, and a silence fell upon us that stayed hard for weeks.

It was about two months later that my father walked into the kitchen with a roll of sheet music. "Learn this," he said and picked the notes out on an ancient zither while I went through the words. Within the hour we were on our way to Smedley's.

Smedley had been having trouble with his fires and the shop was full of hungry, muttering customers. My father pulled into position the lemonade box that served as a platform for the odd singer or reciter who might volunteer to help pass on the time during a lull in the chip trade.

My father called for silence. When he got it he said, very significantly: "Now first we'll have that song about Caruso from my youngest boy, who is a peerless boy alto."

"Who?" asked Smedley.

"My son, the boy Chaliapine."

"No, no. Who is the song about, did you say?"

"Caruso, the peerless Enrico Caruso."

Smedley's hands left the chipper and he moved towards my father.

"Oh aye, of course. He's dead, isn't he?"

"The song my son is going to sing is a small obituary ballad written to lament the passing of the great tenor. Now then, up on this box with you, boy."

I was helped up on to the box that had once contained lemonade bottles. I liked singing on this box. It gave me a sense of authority to be clearly above the heads of my audience, and the empty box gave my voice an extra edge of resonance. I began to sing:

> They needed a song-bird in heaven
> To sing while the angels did play.
> God told the angels where one could be found
> So they came and they took him away.
> He's gone to the sweet land of sunshine
> For ever and ever to stay.
> They needed a song-bird in heaven
> So they took poor Caruso away.

(Copyright Mills Music, Ltd.)

I ended on a note that made four people duck and the metal that covered the counter to rattle. Smedley's face was humble and distraught. "Please sing that again."

We watched Smedley. The words or the sound of my voice had started some gusher of uproarious feeling in him. He had abandoned all his work at the chipper and the pans and was staring through the shop window, uncurtained for greater economy, at the full moon that had just cleared the top of the west mountain.

Smedley scooped the chips and fish into the central compartment of the range. He began to serve. When we offered money he said "Take them, take them. To-night I want no money. Please!"

The word slipped forth and a queue formed outside the shop.

"And keep singing," my father told me. "Keep singing loud."

"Could I switch to 'Roses of Picardy'?" I asked between verses. "I won a prize with 'Roses of Picardy.' "

"Forget roses. Forget Picardy. Keep singing that song about Caruso." And he turned to me and said I was to keep singing that number even if it meant supplying me with air from the back as one did with the more rudimentary chapel organs.

"That boy is hitting some nerve in Smedley with that song. I'm glad of that. Can you imagine those angels just ordering Caruso from God like a meal? We want a song-bird, they say, and off goes this poor Italian. No tenor is safe."

Then when Smedley could give no more away, he went into the kitchen behind the shop and removed his chip coat. He took off the black tie, which he wore as part of the fundamental act of mourning his life had become, and put on a smart bow-tie. It was a floppy red

article of a sort not seen before in Meadow except on the screen of
Luther Cann's cinema, the Coliseum, being worn by such voters as
painters off on some errand of seduction. It gave Smedley a sharply
confidential and sinful look, and we awarded him, as we crowded
around him, full marks for elegance and daring. It was something
the zone had been starved of for years, and we had never thought
to see it around the neck of Smedley. We felt the whole evening take
on an extra pair of wings.

Smedley left the shop. He made no effort to turn us out or to turn
down the lights. This was in clear contrast with his normal practice.
Usually at the end of the day's trading he would be heard for
minutes on end rattling the bolts of his locked door to prove their
firmness, and leaving the shop as utterly lightless and sealed as an
expensive tomb. He had left a pair of cutlets and a modest pile of
chips in the central compartment of the range. At that moment of
ecstatic repletion none of us would have dreamed of laying a finger
on them.

Smedley made his way up The Slope towards the widow's house.
I, following at about ten yards, was still singing but with an ex-
cessive throatiness now and flagging plainly. My classmate, Enzo
Fosco, the son of the Italian caterer, Pietro Fosco, and a boy who
wore his extraordinary perception of things as easily as an old coat,
came quietly up to me and said that my father's intention was to
have me wind up carrying my larynx in a sling.

We all stopped outside the widow's house. Smedley spoke no
word of objection to our following behind him like a long excited
tail. He went at a confident trot to the widow's door. He rapped on
it. The night was quite silent. The three raps on the knocker were
the only marks on it. The sense of high drama we all felt was around
us, tangible as an iron hoop. A dim light came up through the
fanlight above the widow's door. The glass was thick with dust and
seemed consciously to be fighting to put transparency in its flippant
place. From behind the door there was a strange rustle as of some-
one rising from a bed of old newspapers. The door opened. Smedley
asked for the widow's hand. He used a formula as precise as his
moustache, as glaring as the light in his eye. The widow gave a short
sob of acknowledgment and said yes.

We all raised a small cheer and Smedley led the widow down the
hill, adjusting the red bow tie which some convulsion of excitement
had loosened. We reached the shop and my father hurried to get to

the head of the procession.

Smedley and the widow sat down at the table in the chip shop. They were not allowed to lift a finger at their betrothal feast. We put the cutlets and chips left by Smedley on plates, and salted and vinegared them to a point that seemed to please Smedley but startled the widow, who had never before been waited on by so intrusive and eager a corps of helpers, and who had clearly never before seen her chips afloat so soon after their appearance on the plate. We formed a half-circle around the couple and sang them the Hunter's Chorus from *Der Freischutz* which we had just learned at school, and which seemed to have just the note of bounding brightness to set Smedley right for the night.

As we left them Smedley and the widow were exchanging a whole curriculum of glances, grimaces and smiles associated with the urge to be as one. As we walked up the road my father said he was going to call in at Naboth Kinsey's to canonise his gramophone. The moon stood in full and massive censure above our scurrying.

Smedley and the widow were married a week later. They spent their honeymoon at a spa whose waters were very acrid and favoured by Smedley. He returned with the expression of having been laved in a fundamental and not altogether pleasant way. His behaviour in the shop slipped back on to its old granitic base. Caruso himself, giving out with everything he had and helped out by Zenatello, could not have shifted him. He expanded his business. He gave even smaller helpings, put the price of his cutlets up by a half-penny and reduced their size to the point where he seemed to be wishing to hide the identity of the original fish. And he seemed to find some joy in working his wife to death.

One night my father hoisted me once more on to the lemonade box and told me to let rip with the Caruso ballad, while he and his companions hummed a descant. Smedley listened to us for a minute putting a finger in the ear he had nearest to the bubbling chip fat to give us fuller attention. My father watched him attentively, convinced by Smedley's raptness that another moonburst was on its way to Smedley. But all he did was to shout at his wife to hurry with the next bucket of potatoes, and to tell us that if we and our ambitions as a glee group were not out of his shop in thirty seconds he would send for Police Constable Ophie Pinfold, by local standards a mailed fist, and have us charged with creating confusion and migraine in the chip trade.

Smedley's wife came in from the kitchen with a bucket loaded to the brim. He reproved her with clicking teeth and a frozen eye when one potato slid to the floor. She came over to the chipping machine near which my father was standing.

"You and your something Caruso," she said softly. "You and your something moonlight!" A tidy tongue, the widow's, always this side of the uncouth. Then she brought down the blade of the chipper with a homicidal violence and resolve which never again allowed my father to look at or think of chips in the same old tender light.

The Putters-Out

I do not think that the fire brigade in the Meadow Prospect of my youth reached the level of frank skullduggery displayed by the Constantinople Fire Brigade in the days when that body was widely known as one of the least stable elements in the whole jumpy situation of the Levant. With them there were two problems: first to get the flames out; then to do as much for the wildly looting members of the fire-fighting force.

The Meadow Prospect boys were a small body, and for all the hints of bravado that glinted from their helmets, a fairly shy lot. Technically they were the most rudimentary outfit in the history of the hosepipe. Their equipment: a pump of Archimedian cut; hatchets; and some ladders they loaded onto a cart. For a short time they had a horse to drag this cart, and this was the golden age of ease in the experience of the firemen. Then a man, frowning, turned up from nowhere and fetched the horse back, and the brigade had to resume the old regime of hauling and pushing. Meadow Prospect was poor terrain for this sort of exercise. It was a complex of terrifying slopes and all the fires seemed to take place at the top of one of the hills.

It was as if, beyond a certain altitude, people became numb or flippant with height and took a more cordial view of arson. It was a terrible thing to see the brigade manhandle their cart up a slope of two in three. The older and feebler members would give in halfway up the hill and sit the fire out, gasping by the roadside.

Their chief was Abel Holman, a grey, austere, loveless sort of man. Taken in conjuction with the desolation caused by the average blaze, he did much to dispirit the borough. Holman was a roadsweeper by calling and he had ways of looking at you as he did this job that made you feel that if you had stayed indoors the avenue would have been a lot more trim and he would have been saved a lot of wear and tear on his brush. As a sideline he was also the executioner of the area's unwanted dogs, and the quality of his eyes, as they settled on some loose and bounding hound, tore our hearts with a sense of the transience of love and the odds against joy.

The brigade had no uniforms, save the helmets. They marched out to duty in their oldest suits, scuffed enough not to resent any fall of ash or ember. This gave them a look so dowdy that if it had not been for the distant eruption of smoke and flame to put them in context they would have looked like a platoon of low-level refugees wheeling their belongings out of some shattered town. Holman wore the suit one associates with naval warrant officers and this was the nearest the brigade ever got to having an official tone. But their helmets were remarkable. Holman never revealed where he got them but he had clearly pulled off the ironmongering coup of the decade. The average member of the brigade was small and this deepened the impression of the troupe being pinned beneath a vast metal canopy. But the helmets were valued. After half a century of flat caps, bowlers and nothing at all, the helmets were greeted as an uproarious bit of panache. Some of the members wore them on purely civilian errands, such as love-making, to stiffen their confidence and over-awe their companions.

When a fire started, Holman announced it by ringing a handbell. The square, in which the firecart was parked, would fill with bronze. We would cheer as the men began their uphill push. But after a few minutes of propelling the cart along the rutted roads they would shed their glamour and put their helmets on the cart, glowering at Holman and asking him if he had any specific grudge against the idea of having fires in the level part of town where they could get to the blaze at an impressive gallop.

For years they were unpaid. Then it was decided that they should get a shilling an hour from the time they left the square to the time they got back there. That was when my father joined. His first motive was simple greed, for the firemen, by some monstrous bits of dawdling on their way to and from the fires, managed to extend the working period and the fee impressively.

On the flip-side of the greed was a lecture on Nietzsche he had heard delivered in the Institute by the king of local misanthropes, a man who had abandoned compassion as a tactic and was spreading as much spiritual mischief as he could before the Institute Committees caught his drift and walled him up. He had convinced my father that he needed the rough, rude touch of danger to give him a rounded mind. So off he went to Holman to ask how things stood on the helmet front. Holman had one. He had a stock that would have impressed Krupp.

It was a big moment when my father first walked into the kitchen wearing his helmet. He walked very slowly, as if he were moving into a new dimension. He told us later that wearing any kind of metal hat cast an odd spell over his muscles. He sat thoughtfully in his chair. He did not remove his helmet. Now and then he would flick it with his fingers, making a sombre chime as if suggesting to us that with him now in the front line of perilous public service the old serenities of the past were dead and gone. He also read out to us bits from a leaflet, written without enthusiasm by Holman, on how to minimise the danger of publicly significant fires.

He was with Holman for about three weeks. Much anger had been caused by tales of the firemen having lengthened the life of fires by active chicane. They had been seen, said their critics, dragging their feet as they pushed the cart upward to the line of duty. They had waited for fires to get a really adult grip before going into action. It was ruled that only the hours actually spent fire-fighting should be paid for. My father turned out just once. When he heard Holman's handbell, he put on his helmet and touched us all affectionately on the shoulder, as if asking us to see that his memory was kept fresh. I heard him mutter a wish that the fire would be squarely in the house of the man whom he had first heard mention Nietzsche, Holman and helmets.

He took his place behind the cart. He began the long uphill push. It struck us, who were walking on the flanks, that the other firemen, as a form of protest, had withdrawn from this part of the exercise. If the cart was moving at all, my father was the motive power. By the time he reached the fire he was bent, groaning and rubbing his stomach walls. He needed only a few whiffs of smoke to complete his ruin and he got those instantly. He lost all sense of direction. Holman had to spin him clean around twice to keep his waterjet in contact with the flames. Twice he let us have the water, mistaking the radiant interest in our faces for the blaze itself.

The fire was unduly prolonged. It turned out later that two of the more bitter fire-fighters had nipped around the back and thrown a freshly delivered load of coal into the flames to make their errand worthwhile. Holman's brigade was disgraced and disbanded. And I never heard my father mutter a word of complaint.

Nothing To Declare

My father had just one short zoological phase. After brooding and muttering about the blindness and malice of the local council for a good twenty years, he decided that it would be murderous folly to withhold his insight any longer from municipal affairs.

"Until now," he said, "I have been a theorist and critic. A mere juggler with ideas. Not enough. I'm going to stand at the next election. And when I join the senators, just watch. The educational eye will brighten and refuse will be whipped off to the incinerator before it hits the ground. The voters, for the first time, will have the sense of living in a clean and purposive world."

We went along to the meeting at which the candidate of my father's chosen party was to be elected.

My father's name was proposed by his friend, Waldo Treharne. My father stood up smiling and gave a short bow as if apologising to the audience for having kept them waiting so long for a chance to vote him in. The chairman waved my father back into his seat.

"All right. We can see you. Now who'll second that?"

We noticed that it seemed to take an unnaturally long time to find a seconder. When a man stood up to do the seconding he was looking and nodding his head at a man who was not my father. The only people who were looking at my father were moving their lips around phrases that sounded to us like "Irresponsible loon" and "Don't defile the vote."

There were eleven candidates. My father, with a formidable gap of votes between him and the next man, came eleventh.

The following day he called us around him and there was a great bloom of sadness on his face. He waved his arm to take in the whole of Meadow Prospect.

"That lot," he said; "A man belabours his brain with the problems of his time until it shines like a torch. He pushes his skull forward to hint that they could do with a little of his light. The next thing you know they've slipped a snuffer over his wick and passed a fresh vote of confidence in the dark. I'm going to cure you of worry about mankind."

We stepped back, thinking he was going to take some short and rabid cut to this end.

"I'm going to give you a new dimension of interest. I'm going to encourage you to keep pets. I've noticed that people who keep pets tend to be jocose, uncaring. They wouldn't give a damn if humanity were totally enchained if the chains were sixty per cent dog biscuit. What kind of pets do you fancy? We'll make a modest start and keep on until you are on so friendly a footing with the animal world that when you reach twenty-one you will spurn the vote and opt for membership of the local fox-hunting outfit. Now, name your pets."

"Dogs. Cats. They're well known."

"I don't know. Don't like the sound of dogs. Very witless, the bark of a dog. And cats, egomaniacs. Dogs and cats know too much about us. They look as if they'll be around any day now to collect dues and make new rules. And avoid the larger type of animal. Knew a mine owner once. Very wealthy. Mentally unhinged. Had a phobia about the impending revolution. Bought a big camel. Claimed he only felt secure riding about lodged between the two humps. Many short Celts riding camels in sandy places in the Great War had all the fun taken out of a conflict for them by the height and sadness of these animals. No, your first step into the magic world of pets will be modest."

It was. My father came in one day with an unusually small and listless budgerigar in a cage that looked as if one modest peck from the bird would bring it down in ruin. We took that to be the reason why the bird sat so still. One false vigorous move and it would have found itself emeshed in a tangle of girders.

"This bird is the king of songsters, the Lloyd George of budgerigars. Our only problem will be to get it to shut up and let us get in a word edge-wise. What will we call him?"

We came out with some of the more obvious names. "Poll," "Joey," and so on. My father raised one leg as if wishing to step out of this swill of banality. His eyes grew very bright. At that period he had his head up a flue of Welsh legend, and his eyes had developed this way of lighting up to suggest the approach of high and ancient romance.

"We'll call him Gwalchmai."

"Who's Gwalchmai?"

"One of the Arthurian group, a noted battler. And if we decide to enter this bird for the vocal section of the Caged Bird show, we'll give him his full title. 'Gwalchmai of Caerleon-on-Usk.'

We suggested that a name as jaw-cracking as Gwalchmai would drive the bird into the arms of the Trappists or a fast moult.

"Listen," said my father. "This bird was reared in a part of Wales where budgerigars learn to articulate at Eisteddfod level. Don't underestimate the intelligence of budgies. That's what we've done with humans and look where that's landed us. Now then, let's give this bird it's identity."

He stood squarely in front of the bird and said, "I am Gwalchmai of Caerleon-on-Usk."

We said in low voices that Gwalchmai might be happier with a simple tag like, "I am Percy from Ponty," or "I am Billy from Baglan."

"No," said my father. "Budgies like the underprivileged and caged everywhere await a challenge. I've heard people who've been content with budgies that say such things as, 'Silly boy,' 'Dirty Dick,' and a few oaths and even slower types of nursery rhyme."

He tried again.

"Now then, I am Gwalchmai of Caerleon-on-Usk."

Gwalchmai's eyes frosted over and he turned right around to face the nearest wall.

But my father did not give up.

"Perhaps this is a kind of modest budgie that doesn't like announcing itself brazenly. We'll try him with some general statements."

He treated Gwalchmai to a round of these: "Milton, thou should'st be living at this hour." "Shelley! whose song so sweet was sweetest here," and one of his own: "Through every war emerges one more fragment of peace's eventual face."

Gwalchmai looked as if he might start arguing about that, but my father repeated it in Welsh and Gwalchmai went back to staring at the wall.

After a few days of this my father said, "It's the cage that's keeping him dumb. It's the indignity of that wire. We'll let him out. Don't worry. He's been listening to me. I know that. He's got a whole libretto of stuff in that little yellow head, and once he starts flying about, landing on our heads and hands, he'll be belting it out non-stop."

He opened the cage. Gwalchmai came out like a torpedo, took a swift peck at my father, flew through the window and headed straight for England.

The Stammering Hammer

My father functioned as a hinge between two ages that yawned so swiftly away from each other it was little wonder his face bore a look of gaping strain during the later part of his life.

The Industrial Revolution left no one in deeper doubt than he was. One day he would be deploring the manual toil in which all his life had been spent, and his tongue would start pushing us upward to the peak of academic achievement. When at the age of nine I was crying out for the second volume of Tiger Tim, he gave me a copy of Kant's *Critique of Pure Reason*, and the nearest he came to try sweetening the pill was to mumble an apology for having failed to get me the edition with pictures.

"Stick with Kant," he said. "You'll find the going cruelly rough beneath your feet but what is a sore toe when you know you are going to come back with a basketful of truth? Imagine the pictures for yourself."

This I tried to do and it accounts for the piece in the back of my mind that stays turned up to this day.

"Words, words," he would tell us. "Words are the ladder out of the hole and hovels that have been laid down as a trap for the slow and the gentle. And let the words get longer. That way you'll keep the world foxed, in awe. Do not be judged. Slip on the wig and make your own judgments."

But there were moments when his faith in the higher literacy faltered. When he saw our obsession with books making us more and more inept in manual affairs, he would tut-tut and quote general Gerald Winstanley the Digger who condemned all intellectuals as "Monsters, all tongue and no hand." "Men will always find ways of dishing the mind. Can I be sending you forth defenceless, more crooked beneath a weight of useless knowledge than ever I was beneath the outrage of the mining caper."

Then he would go on to tell us of the delight he had found in the many crafts he had practised. If one could believe, he had been a sort of Michelangelo: tiler, bricklayer, plasterer, carpenter, glazier, painter. The only thing we had ever known him to be was an ostler, tending pit ponies, and the only thing he had ever described in his traffic with these animals was the speed at which he bolted along the dark tunnels when the horses grew fractious and banded against his way of dispensing the oats.

"I will restore the magic to your hands," he said. "I want you to be balanced men. If ever you land in a wilderness you can punctuate your mutilations with a bit of creative craftsmanship."

We waited for the exhibition to start, but there was no stir of nail or hammer.

Then we got hold of the rabbits. There were two of them left loose in a garden by a neighbour called Price, who had done a flit from a siege of bailiffs. We brought them home. My father looked at them coldly. We remembered him saying that rabbits had a depressing smell. "We'll eat them," he said. There was some crisis of shortage going on at the time and my father was fond of coming out with these curt, Malthusian directives.

"Oh, no," we said. "We want to keep them, we want to feed them and love them."

He looked at us as if we were starting some new perversion and he put on the look he always wore when he wondered what had planted such a hedge between him and the diaconate.

"They are a buck and a doe," we said. "They are called Ollie and Dollie."

He asked us to repeat this. He suspected that whenever we gave names to anything or anybody we fresh-minted them just to astonish him

We took a closer look at the rabbits. They were two of the weariest seeming animals we had seen. It was clear that during the few days before Price, our neighbour, had turned his back on the bailiffs, he had not given much thought to the diet of Ollie and Dollie.

We reminded my father of the many talks he had given us on creative craftsmanship.

"We want you to make us a hutch."

He stood quite still, looking absorbed, as if mentally choosing between a dozen blueprints.

"I'll have to find some wood," he said and left the house. When he came back we agreed that no man had ever left a house specifically for wood and come back with less. "Wood's pretty tight," he said.

We searched around for hammers and nails. During my father's exile from the crafts he had allowed his materials to become very dispersed.

He began the nailing. He used the pincers a lot. He never seemed to attach one piece of wood to another without instantly changing his mind. As we were about to challenge his approach and suggest that Ollie and Dollie might as well sleep with us, he said: "That's the mark of the creative craftsman; the second thought, the second view."

The hutch took shape. It seemed very small. "Have you measured Ollie and Dollie? Is that thing going to fit them?"

"I've made it deliberately bijou; keeping them cramped will keep their mind off whatever it is that worries rabbits when they are hopping about loose. They will concentrate more on the human element around them and they will give you a warmer affection." He was now taking a closer interest in the rabbits. "Ollie and Dollie. These two will sire an army. One half will go for food and the other half will be given to voters who appreciate the cuddly side of these animals. A few we will unleash as a plague against those hillside farmers whose attitude I consider sullen. Of course, Ollie and Dollie look a bit under par now. No doubt Price, our neighbour, told them all about his debts before he fled and that must have worried them."

We put the rabbits in the hutch. They were touching and this had nothing to do with fondness. The hutch fitted them like a shirt. Ollie was giving my father a look that rabbits normally keep for snakes.

"We'll keep them in the hutch for a day or two to let them win back the weight and confidence they lost with Price."

We laid odds that after one meal he'd have to tear the hutch from around them to get them loose. The rabbits were now crouching, a posture that one might have expected from rabbits conscious of being in a mining area.

"In that position they'll waste no energy at all. They'll breathe, they'll eat. And the first whiff of freedom they get, it'll be jubilee day even for a creature as prolific as the cony."

The next two days nearly saw Ollie and Dollie over the Jordan. Each of us was convinced that the others had callously forgotten

Ollie and Dollie and their needs. We shuffled furtively as smugglers to the hutch, each bearing a fresh load of greens. Ollie and Dollie were turning up their eyes and groaning. We had half a garden full of cabbages and sprouts and we all felt as liberal as Dickens. We couldn't hand out the stuff fast enough. Whatever sounds rabbits make when they are asking to see their consul, these rabbits were making.

Whenever my father passed them he would smile and say that to create even a tiny corner of repletion in a deficient world was its own reward. He spoke of the need for a controlled breeding programme and a super hutch built in superior lasting wood of which he would not be ashamed when rabbit-lovers and research workers came around to study our methods and achievements.

On the fourth day the door of the hutch was open and the rabbits were gone. They might have been stolen. Such simple bits of rustling were not unknown in the area at the time. One of my brothers might have detected symptoms of surfeit in Ollie and Dollie and freed them. The fugitive Price might have come back for them. Or my father might have panicked at the grandeur of his super-hutch fantasy, despaired of ever getting together the time and materials for such a pleasure dome and backed out the easy way. I had heard him say that he didn't like the way Ollie looked at him. Besides my father had great belief in the virtues of his home-grown cabbage. In his day he was a precocious fan of the vitamin and the way Ollie and Dollie were going they would have converted the back garden into a small Sahara within a month. Anyway, after the rabbits had gone he looked a lot more normal.

The Welsh Dreamer

I have never seen a stoat mesmerise a rabbit. Only once did I ever see these two animals in confrontation and they did not seem to be up to anything very much. It was in the middle of a most bleak and discouraging summer and there was a religious revival of medium wattage going on in Meadow Prospect which tended to cool villainy and fortify the meek. So, between the weather and the emotional rumpus, the stoat and the rabbit might have been thrown out of their normal stride. But I did see my father and Idwal Ford, and that was every bit as good.

Idwal was the most responsive and suggestible lad in our stretch of the valley. And my father was his Pied Piper. Just one hint of a note and Idwal came running to the colours. Specially in the matter of the Welsh and their place and identity in the world.

For most of his life my father had been content with beer, sensual pleasure and general debate. About his national label he was, for a long time, off-hand. He was born in America. His father, an altruist and recessive to a fault, had taken a vow that he would never stand in the way of America's drive to world power, and he came back to Aberdare to be out of Theodore Roosevelt's way. He bought a shaky stake in a dying carpentry business and sent it galloping to the tomb. His main thought had been that in America his sons would have lost the Welsh language and the Welsh had lost enough already. My father stayed neutral and willingly mobile.

But in the 'fifties my father's Welshness sprang back to life. By this time he had offended most of his children and whenever he came in our kitchen filled with a sullen silence. All of his children had forgotten the Welsh language. My father could still speak it, and used it as a club to beat us with.

We did not listen. Idwal Ford did. No rabbit ever turned up for his hypnotic shot more readily than Idwal. Every Welsh hero who had ever lived, from Llewellyn Bren, who was beheaded in Cardiff by sadistic Normans, to Mabon, the miners' leader, who was insulted in Parliament by sneering Etonians, danced on my father's tongue. Idwal listened entranced and committed the names and stories of the Celtic banner-bearers to heart.

My father made a cult of Welsh rugby. This game, he told Idwal, represented the genius of the Cymro in defence and attack. He would give Idwal a blow-by-blow account of the match in 1905 when Wales defeated the All-Blacks. He persuaded him to take up the game. Idwal had no gift for it. He had neither speed nor strength, but after a wide-eyed session with my father he was convinced that he had the agility of Nureyev, the floating Slav, and Nurmi, the Flying Finn. "Idwal," said my father, "you were born to wear the red jersey of Wales."

Idwal got one match with the Prospect Pumas. He played against a ferocious set called the Trecysgod Terrors who were said to field no fewer than four disguised and unregistered Dacoits in every game. Idwal kept interrupting his futile bursts of play with appeals to all the players to respect the sacred Welsh concept of pure justice, robust thrusts but nothing dirty. He was kicked twice by the referee who wished to be the only orator on view, and clobbered repeatedly by the other twenty-nine players. He took up bowls, also, according to my father, a fine game, pinched from the Welsh by Drake, an English pirate.

My father bought a picture from the Birchtown market called "Owain Glyndwr at Dusk". Owain was a Welsh aristocrat who at the end of the fourteenth century led a rebellion which left a lot of people bewildered and a lot of places charred. The picture showed him in his last phase as a fugitive. His face is sadder than night as he stares at mist on distant hills. "The typical Welshman," said my father. "Broken, after brave rebellion, in despair, but knowing that one day from the mountains and valleys of a great rebirth, the day of Welsh restitution will arise."

Idwal was bewitched by this image. He took to standing on the mountain top above our street, wearing a long, shabby raincoat, the nearest he could come to the cloak worn by Glyndwr in the picture, and staring in every direction for signs of the great Welsh counter-coup. He ran into trouble. Lovers who used the plateau had been complaining for months of a crazed watcher, a voyeur who kept them under constant observation and looked as if he might one day soon switch from simple spying to maniacal assault. Idwal was interviewed by the police and warned to mend his ways and buy a new mac to see if that would take his mind off the Saxon foe.

Five years running Idwal submitted a poem to the Meadow Prospect Eisteddfod. The poems hardly varied in form. They always began: "Now, Welshmen, let us stem the tide/Of Cymru's woes and humbled pride." In each version the Welsh were likened to some national group suffering persecution in this part of the world or some other: Red Indians, gypsies, Bengalis, Eskimos, homosexuals and sex-changers. They were all grist to Idwal's paranoiac mill. Some of the rhymes were startling. One poem ended: "Why, my angry Welsh soul asks/Are we not in arms with the gallant Basques?" After his fifth try, two out of the three adjudicators suggested that they should give Idwal a consolation prize for effort. The third adjudicator agreed that this should be done, provided that the prize be something tonic and curative like liver-pills, and wrapped in a one-way ticket to Zimbabwe where Joshua Nkomo might be needing a bard with a fresh angle and pencil-power to last him out to the end of the century.

Idwal was in our kitchen some time back wanting me to sign a petition for Instant Devolution. He also had the opening lines of a new poem: "Let the ugly Saxon hog now grunt and bristle/Confronted by the leek, the shamrock and the thistle."

He had trouble with the Welsh language. It is a monstrously difficult tongue and Idwal, like most other humans, is stretched to the limit by handling just the one language he has always known. He has signed up for three crash-courses in Welsh, and in each case the tutor, a man of missionary zeal, has advised Idwal to stick to any form of agitation that can be done in total silence. Idwal went off and daubed a wall with stinging rebuke in whitewash to people who were dragging their feet over devolution. His face grew quite distorted after his fracas with the crash-courses. Partly it was disappointment, partly the strain of trying to fit his lips, teeth and throat around the tricky range of Welsh sounds. To compensate, he changed his name from Ford to the more Welsh-looking Ffordd. An anti-Welsh neighbour, alarmed by this spawning of consonants in a time that called for economy, wrote him a note, advising him to "buzzz offf".

If all swimmers against the tide of public apathy had as little luck as Idwal, this would be a quiet world. But he has a genius for putting his foot into any nest of misunderstanding that happens to be around. He attended a local meeting to celebrate the anniversary of the return to Parliament of three Nationalist MPs. He recalled something that my father had said years before: "When we send our own men to Westminster, they should wear the fine distinctive costume of the Druids. Sweeten the fetid air of that sty of compromise and betrayal with the bracing wind of Cymric poetry. No lounge suits for Welsh patriots." Idwal blurted this out. The chairman, a convert from the Labour Party, and still tending to be a bit schizoid and morose in his political brooding, accused Idwal of being an anti-Welsh satirist and ordered him out of the meeting, and told two Simon-pure lovers of the red dragon to keep an eye on him.

Idwal was depressed about that for weeks. But the National Eisteddfod comes round every year. Once he gets a fresh headful of those trumpeters summoning the victorious bard from his shy darkness, Idwal's heart will be riding over the hills again with Glyndwr and Tommy Thomas of Penygraig, a light heavyweight who wrestled hills as part of his training, bathed only in icy mountain streams, died young and left behind him a hush of wonder and pity that still causes the wind to pause at odd moments around the mountains. And behind Idwal, guiding the steed of ancient dreams to a higher and higher glory, will be my father's elfin ghost.

A Thought For The Dragon

My father, at moments of inward cold, was capable of wearing the Welsh past like a flaming and terrible garment. His mind and tongue were drawn most passionately to the lurid and twilight of Roman rule in Britain.

"Think, think," he would say, "of Cunedda the Burner."

"What did he burn?"

"Anything."

"What was he burning for?"

"Wrath. He played hell with the Romans in Northern Britain. Cunedda was a Pict. There has been a lot of loose, libellous talk about the Pict. Ignore it. Cunedda was a Pict. Night after night, from their fortresses and their walls, the Romans looked at the reddening sky of their doom. Cunedda was at the torch again."

My father would end this phase of the story thus. "One day it will be proven that King Arthur the Peerless was really Cunedda the Burner and the Picts will come into their own again."

He became gently lyrical about Saint David, "The holy Dewi at whose passing the sun sank at noon and all humanity wept." For years he promised us a trip to St David's cathedral. "I will show you the relics, the actual bones of this holiest of men who walked the earth in a dawn of goodness."

We made the trip in a charabanc so old and unsprung it gave a mediaeval note to the whole pilgrimage. A fog started at Carmarthen and deepened by the minute. My father put this down to the English who were out to baulk any effort by the Welsh to set eyes on the relics of their patron saint and scholar. By the time we reached the headland of Saint David about the only thing we could see was the gleaming starch of my father's winged collar. We foxed various villagers by walking into their cottages demanding to be shown the relics.

Many incidents from the far past seemed to find a unique mouth in my father. History glowed through him to the point where he ceased to be a puzzled man in a broken town and one saw only a skeleton of remembrance. He was very good on Gruffydd the Second, the prince who tried to keep afloat in the first wave of the Norman conquest. He could recite the names of the first great border-barons as a kind of black and sour litany. Hugo the Wolf, The Norman Earl of Chester, Robert of Rhuddlan and the rest. He would often visit the castles of Ludlow, Chester, Ross, where the captive Celts were once treated to courses of fetters, hot oil, eye-gouging and worse.

"And worse. Nameless were the things those French and Saxon rogues did to our men and nameless they shall remain."

This disappointed us, for we had stomachs strong as brass for horror.

"Do not ever forget Meirion Goch, Meirion the Red. No, no, I do not mean Meirion Pugh the Anarcho-Syndicalist from Bedwas Road who is also called Meirion the Red. This Meirion I'm talking about has been dead for close on a thousand years, and not a day too short for my money. He was the rodney who betrayed Gruffydd into the hands of Hugo the Wolf, who was a friend of Robert of Rhuddlan. Gruffydd lay for six years in Chester, in chains and the iron made a meal of his flesh. He was rescued by Cynric Hir, Cynric the Tall, a young chieftain who crossed the Dee with the lacerated Gruffydd on his back. For years Gruffydd wandered. Gruffydd walked even further. More uphill. He was known as Gruffydd the Wanderer."

There was a local man called Hughes the Totterer, an erratic, cider-drinking marathon walker whose face we conjured up at every mention of Gruffydd.

"Gruffydd raided the castle of Robert of Rhuddlan at Deganwy. They met face to face, Gruffydd and Robert. The Welshman won and he sailed away, his ship full of the Norman's sleek, black cattle and on the top of his mast...guess what?"

We all knew. But we'd make a few guesses just to stoke my father's passion up a few degrees. "A flag." "The Red Dragon rampant with pride." "The jerkin of a fallen foe."

"No!" And my father's smile would be devilish under his moustache, grown very bushy to remind us of Lloyd George.

"Nailed to the mast was the head of Robert of Rhuddlan. I am against nailing, thinking it a crude and noisy tactic. A nice bit of quiet dove-tailing is the very summary of love as I see it. But on that occasion, there at far Deganwy, Gruffydd could have trusted me with the hammer."

Places where blatant anti-Welsh treachery had happened were never, for my father, quite disinfected. "Take Abergavenny. Had many a charabanc outing to Abergavenny. Nice, pleasant, harmless-seeming place. Enjoyed it. But that was before I read about Iorwerth ab Owen. This took place in the reign of Henry the Second, who was a knock to Becket and a serious nuisance to the Celt. Under a flag of truce Iorwerth came to visit the castle at Abergavenny, whose lord was William de Breos of Brecknock, and if you cannot hear villainy in that man's name you have not been getting my message. With Iorwerth to Abergavenny came Sesyll ap Dunwal and the rest of his kinsmen. De Breos had provided a feast and the dessert was hard and bitter. Around the banqueting hall were stationed a ring of butchers under the command of Ranulf Poer, the sheriff of Hereford, and that's another place you can keep your eye on. Hereford. At a signal the Norman wolves ravened in and massacred the unarmed guests. So, don't forget, Abergavenny. Next time you go there and call in anywhere, say, for a cup of tea, keep your eyes wary and wide-open. And whether you go there by bus or train, keep your fingers on your return ticket."

Builth Wells was another place perpetually dark for my father. It was near Builth, "near the little church of Llanynys beside the dark Yrvon" that Llewellyn the Last was betrayed and slain. He would show us a coloured picture of the last prince, standing by the ford, his hair golden, a short, futile sword in hand, wearing a scarlet tunic and a blue cloak and his face pained as an armoured knight puts a lance through his chest. It was a river bank where broom grew in profusion.

"Go to the spot and the people will tell you that no broom has ever grown again in Llanganten parish from that dark day to this, not until recently anyway. I've tried to be fair to Builth. More than once I've had various disorders of the lower bowels put right by taking heavy draughts of its harsh and purgative spa-water. I had been brooding about Llewellyn the Last and Builth's undoubted complicity in his death. I went into the pump room. I took my usual heavy swig of the liberating stuff. My bowels did not stir. They probably thought, as I did, that it would have been treachery to the ghost of Llewellyn to react in the usual squalid way. I doubled the dose and the supervisor set two attendants to watch me and declared a state of emergency.

A great eruptive grief filled me. I left the pump-room with the feeling that I was shortly going to fall apart. I walked to the stream-side spot where the great Llewellyn and the broom in which he stood had died. The Builth waters sprang like Normans to the kill. I shook hands with Llewellyn."

My father's trip through our bloody patch of national time ended with Owen Glyndwr. "Blessed is he whose death in the minds of his compatriots is an end and a beginning. Listen!" He would put his head on one side and open his mouth wide to provide a kind of radar trap for all the mysterious, elusive sounds that come out to us from the perished past. He would tell all of us to do the same. We did so. We tilted our heads and dropped our jaws excessively. To a passing eye, we must have looked like the finest gallery of dolts ever organised.

"Listen! You will hear him as he passes furtively through the hills during those last terrible years. Hunted, heart-broken, hurt in mind and body. There is no valley in the land through which he can pass without seeing or sensing the endless graves of comrades slain. He carried the death of a nation upon his back. He fashioned for his soul a unique torment. Is it any wonder then that he did not completely die, that he waits even now beneath a friendly and lightly-poised rock for the moment of recall. He may be lying at Ogof y Ddinas, a cave well to the west of here, an area where the high wages in the anthracite industry and an obsession with rugby football will have dropped Owen to the bottom of the agenda. The only real significance that Ogof y Ddinas has today is that from this cave is obtained some type of dust or powder which is used in the making of false teeth. This puts Owen into a poor light, and marks one of the most serious declensions of glory even in our own jerky annals. But he'll be back. He'll be back to twit the local councillors on the failure to curb a rising rate and end the scandal of that burning tip at the bottom of Bethesda Row which gives out flames and a smell evil enough to make the grave seem a wholesome proposition. He'll be back to censure Lloyd George for having allowed himself to become the pawn of warlords and for having extended needlessly the area of Welsh participation in world butchery. He'll be back to trip up the schemes of those clowns who want to shore up the walls and refill the moat of Caerphilly Castle, that badge of national disgrace, though I see that a brisker tourist trade to the restored fortress might offset the eclipse of the cheese trade in that area. That's how it is. You start with Cunedda the Burner and you wind up with cheese."

The Appeal

Just before I went up to Oxford on the smallest grant in the history of official caution, I was discussing with my brothers how, short of open banditry and a swoop on the Council Chamber, we might supplement the pittance.

"What about Perry?" asked Dil, "Perry the grocer?" His voice had an edge of mischief and we didn't blame him.

This Perry was a shopkeeper on the other side of the river, a violent curmudgeon. He was related to us by marriage. He figured largely in my father's private myth. It was believed in the family that my grandfather had left a lot of money. He had built houses here and there in the village, mainly in treacherous beds of peat and they sank a foot as soon as the first tenant moved in and exerted any kind of serious pressure on the floorboards.

Most of the tenants disappeared: either through debt or a genuine journey through the top-soil. He was also an undertaker for a year that was good for death, and it was said that he had twice drowned the diminuendo bits of 'The Messiah' in an adjoining chapel with the rattle of his hammer on endless coffins. He had come as near to cleaning up as one can in a place where finance was mainly a rumour.

My father said that he and his brother, Denzil, had been active members in the mortuary outfit. He had been the master of a tool called an adze, and he had added, with the aid of this article, many a classic touch to the modest casket popular in the zone. He claimed that after the influenza epidemic of 1907 he had contributed to the last rites of one third of the village's victims, and that those of the dead who had opted for other undertakers had had no taste in wood seen in a context of burial.

My father and Uncle Denzil, given to drink, gambling and lechery, borrowed money from Perry at rates that brought a glow of optimism back to the cheeks of usury in the zone. For every ten pounds they got from Perry they handed him IOUs for thirty. When my grandfather died the exultation of my father and Denzil was high. They made a coffin, filled it with ale, called in a coven of thirsty cronies and drank the lot.

Their joy was brief. They found that what they owed Perry was more than the inheritance. Perry moved in like a panther. He collared what was left of the grandfather's building and undertaking business. My father mourned much over that particular point. He said that he and Denzil had brought a fresh breath of geniality into the doleful business of interment, and when they lost the workshop a lot of the fun had been taken out of death.

The grocer, Perry, figured in our legend as a kind of Sheriff of Nottingham, and my father and Denzil as a conjoint Hood, hounded and stripped by villainy and greed in the days of their innocence. My own contacts with Perry had been few. Now and then I saw him in action at the massive singing events organised on an inter-chapel basis. Perry was steadily in view and clearly audible at these gatherings.

He was a loud tenor, with a way of keeping a jump ahead in the hymn they were currently squeezing the juice out of, leaping on to the next verse like a fearless rider on some Pony Express of piety. He also had a way, while singing, of lifting his eyes to heaven as if to suggest that he was planting his message squarely at the feet of the throne, having no truck with intermediaries. Welsh politicians and presenters are very good at this tactic of supplication through an upward rolling eye.

I have seen meetings of miners being addressed by leaders eager to blow away some bit of suspected duplicity with a few evangelical gusts, invoking aid with their eyeballs from above at such speed that the miners left the meeting in droves, vocationally worried about the safety of the roof.

Seeing Perry in these moods, moving his arms in what he hoped might be a universal embrace, singing away in his accurate tenor, cantering ahead of the congregation to be the first in paradise, spreading sweetness and love over a tremendous surface, I found it hard to connect him with sharp practice. Falling under Perry's spell in those few moments when he stayed calm in your part of the hymnal, it occurred to me that my father's story of the inheritance, the IOUs, the seizure of the undertaking business might well be a pack of lies. It probably was.

Only once was I exposed in any frankly personal way to Perry. I would have been about nine. My father came on to me at the top of the garden. We were standing near the bed of mint planted around the small water-closet to provide a moat of counter-suggestion. He gave me a letter which he wanted me to deliver to Perry. He added in a mutter, "Justice must be done." And when he saw me look confused he muttered it again in slightly fuller form. "I have been wronged and justice must be done."

Ever since that moment muttering for me, has had a flavour of mint. Our teacher at the time was feeding us, in outline, with the story of *The Count of Monte Cristo*. My heart had gone out utterly to Dantès and I was hot for revenge and justice. I could see myself, having slipped the note over, taking two of my brothers as seconds and duelling to the death with Perry for the recovery of my father's lost treasure.

I tingled with excitement as I crossed the bridge that led me into Perry's part of the town. Emotionally it was a big trip. It led over two bridges, one over the river, one over the railway. Both suggested an incursion into regions of strangeness and hostility. The town was divided into communities based on sources of immigration. One would pass through the loamy monotone of the English shire accents into the dramatic gabble of the Welsh. Constantly the people around seemed not to believe that they were actually there.

I found Perry serving a shopful of customers at top speed. His way with groceries was like his way with a hymn. He was always a line ahead of the pack. He was smiling and his hands were moving like magic along the shelves. The sight of me disturbed and angered him. He made some mistakes, giving people ham instead of luncheon roll, which must have annoyed him still further, for he took pride in being a nimble-fingered grocer.

He told me to wait outside and I waited until the shop was empty. In a low and loathing voice he told me to come in. The smell of all that food made me feel hungry, but I felt no urge to mention that to Perry. I gave him the letter. He tore it open as if he wished it were some enemy's flesh. He said, "Oh, he does, does he?"

I am not sure how the situation developed from there, but I found myself shooting out of Perry's shop like a bullet, and Perry was right behind me waving in his hand what I took to be his major bacon knife. Perry, at that moment, was clearly demented and would liked to have satisfied some part of his Bible-fed passion with a bit of living sacrifice.

I had once seen Perry on the stage of the Church Hall, taking the part of Abraham in a cantata about the sacrifice of Isaac. Perry, in a white robe and a mat of cotton wool over his chin and chest to suggest a beard, had Isaac, also in a white robe but clean-shaven, stretched out on a rock and Perry was holding a knife over him. It occurred to me that if the police whipped Perry in for chasing me in this way he would say he was practising and airing his knife for the next cantata.

My foot caught in a loose flagstone and I went flying. Perry ran into me and also plunged out of control. He went one way, his knife another. He was stunned and so was I. In my daze I stayed true to what have always been my favourite impulses, politeness, curiosity and flattery. I picked up the knife, handed it back to Perry and asked him if that was the knife he had used in the cantata, and added that he had been first-rate as Abraham in that beard and robe.

I made the rest of the journey home terrified and limping. My father was still at the top of the garden savouring the effect of the evening air on the mint bed and the rose bushes which flanked it. I told him that Perry had come after me with a knife and seemed to want to murder me.

"I thought he would," said my father sadly. He plucked a rose, a big, rusted tea rose and offered it to me as a kind of balm.

We Are Not Living,
We're Hiding

When history marches forward, I tend to waltz sideways. When the great banners are unfurled. I hide my face in a handkerchief. When the epochal songs are dragged out into the light, I do my finest whistling in the deepest dark. I wish it had been otherwise. I could do with a stronger pride in my past.

These thoughts sprout from the memory of an autumn in the first half of the 1930s. I was a student nursing a stable of thyroidal dreams in the worst apartment in one of Oxford's smaller colleges. Its main room had a low, dark beam against which I enjoyed concussing myself when things became too rugged. On it a laughing sage had written, *Non omnis moriar*. The bedroom had a window that would not close. I stared through it for hours. It overlooked a graveyard, immensely old and untended, which probably accepted its first customer when the college laid its first stone in the fourteenth century. And all around, faces, voices and attitudes that were, to me, as alien as the spiky goblins of science fiction. Compared with the living I found that little plot of human compost tonic. If they had been issuing degrees down there I would have changed the shape of my gown.

Into this gloom landed the letter from my Uncle Edwin. It was a long letter, a good letter. Uncle Edwin was one of the loudest instruments in the brass section of Meadow Prospect's left wing. Reading his message took my mind off a plan I had devised for muffling the odious clanging of the college chapel bell with my bare, protesting head. Uncle Edwin's message was that the valleys wanted to make some sort of gesture against the rheumatoid condition of the national morality and the local trade. Each day a colliery and a chapel would look at each other, wink, laugh and close. Meadow Prospect was contributing a hundred furious marchers to a massive walk of protest to London. The banners were being stitched, feet were being hardened and drummers recruited. Uncle Edwin would be among them, and he looked forward to seeing me in high militant feather on the western approaches to Oxford.

My first impulse on reading the letter was to institute a kind of practice Jacquerie in the ancient town, pinning warning notes to the doors of Heads of Colleges and levying a hot soup tax on every bourgeois under and around the spires. During the next week my mood could not have changed more drastically if Dr Frank Buchman had been feeding live pellets into my porridge. Over the landing from me was one of the most earnest and persuasive Oxford Groupers who ever aired a sin and smiled through breakfast. He had been at me three or four times to fill my hollow, threatening cheeks with goodness and ditch for ever the harsh materialism that made me so fanatical about bread and work, and throw salt over my left shoulder every time I heard a hymn. I was also in the middle of a prize essay on a group of 13th century hagiographers in Aragon. This turned out to be the prescribed topic for the year before, but I don't think I would have made the ratings even if I had consulted the right syllabus. I mention this only to show that there was at that time no level of disorientation in which I was not working all out.

The Oxford Grouper had got me kneeling. The prize essay laid me flat. The day before the marchers arrived my nerves were the rawest part of Europe. I walked out to Godstow and would, without question, have gone into the Thames if the Grouper had not at that moment come hurtling along the towpath brandishing what he thought was a clinching pamphlet.

The marchers arrived the following evening. They were given some rough accommodation in the local hall. I did not see them. I stayed in my room. A neurotic misery was hardening with a geological authority around my heart. About nine I heard a loud Welsh voice coming up from the quadrangle. It was Uncle Edwin asking a college servant if I was there. The servant pointed up at my darkened window and said that showed I must be out. He must be there, said Uncle Edwin. I heard them mount the stairs. I stayed motionless in the bedroom, counting the tombstones in the funeral patch as the door was banged. They went away.

Later, I crept along to the hall where the marchers were lodged. On my way I bought a hot pie from a transport cafe near Carfax.

These pies had a way of slipping an iron collar round my stomach and leading it around like an old serf. It was a chosen way of suffering. The marchers and their well-wishers were singing a good-night rouser, some resurrectionary anthem. I munched my pie and tried to join in. I could not. Shame, the silence and the smell of the shadows, the taste of the off-beat meat, closed in to create the last stain on a remarkably sad autumn.

The next day I left the college at dawn. In an hour I had loped to the peak of Shotover, thinking of Shelley and congratulating him on having known a more refined line to social distress than mine. At about eleven in the morning, I heard, from the direction of Headington Hill, the sound of the four fifes and three drummers who headed the demonstration. I made my way towards them. I tended to hide even when there was no possibility on earth that I would be seen.

I saw them from a side street. I saw Uncle Edwin. He was looking tired and thoughtful. Like many others, he had a limp. He was carrying a banner and making heavy weather of it. It was hanging forward and sheltering the drummers from the drizzle that was falling. They looked as pleased as Burmese monarchs, but Uncle Edwin told me later that the drum-strokes had a paralysing effect on his arms and he had no alternative to letting his banner sag. He had sensitive feet, quick to blister. He said it was just his luck to embrace only causes that called for heavy walking I followed them at a distance of about half a mile, limping in sympathy and wishing that Uncle Edwin would spot me and beat me to death with the banner pole.

I went back to the college. The Grouper was in a dangerous state of exultation. He congratulated me on having refused to be tainted by the scrofula of godless protest. Then he went off to the Bodleian where he had some kind of nervous collapse and destroyed a bust of John Stuart Mill.

Three days late as curt a note as was ever meant to wound told me that I had been placed last in the Essay Prize competition of the year before. My nerves felt as if they had just been sprung from a sweat-box. That night I wandered alone in the Walton Street area and was three times approached by women and thrice confronted by proctors, who would not believe that the women had wheeled and vanished instantly at the sight of my gaunt and evangelical looks.

The following Sunday was the sourest Sabbath I ever knew. The insistent bells, the regimented piety, built up in me a disgust that made Rimbaud a starter. My mood needed a catalyst. It found two: a Yorkshire pudding at lunch that had ossified to a point that had my stomach glaring at me with both Neronian thumbs down, and a fellow-student from Liverpool who was trying to curry favour with the Head of the College by saying that agnostics should be hanged. He was staring so hard at my neck as he said this that he neglected the sirloin of beef on his plate.

I left the lunch halfway through the sweet. I rushed across the High, patted the tomb of Shelley in University College, asked Byron to move up and cadged a lift from the first lorry I saw heading East. It was a furniture lorry going to London. The driver welcomed me into his cab. He was a very literate man. He had heard about the Aztecs who burned their furniture every five years, the regenerative lustrum, and he was all for it. He dropped me at Ealing. I knew little of London. As far as I knew I could have met Uncle Edwin and the marchers at any inch of the way from there on. I kept walking through what I still consider the longest dusk in the whole of crepuscular progression. It was dark when I got to Hyde Park Corner. The place was teeming and in some kind of novel ferment. The marchers were there in force. Under a street lamp of great power I met Uncle Edwin. For at least two minutes we stared at each other. "I was ill, Uncle Edwin," I said. And he said. "My function on this earth, boy, is to believe anything."

Hymn-singing started and Hyde Park Corner had never known such miraculous plangency. We stripped the shrouds off every funeral anthem beloved by the Fringe. We did the dead proud. And within an hour another wonder was unmasked. Every Welsh girl in London had come to do obeisance to the crusade of the ragged and footsore. There were the skivvies and the shop-girls, drawn like bawling moths to the centres of the hot, yearning heart of song. But on the periphery were the corps of Silurian Traviatas who had fled from the scrubbing brush and the till and had taken up the pavement trade. They had that afternoon convened a hasty meeting in a Piccadilly hotel. They were that night to serve the incandescent exiles who flocked down Oxford Street to the hymn-singing. Their fees were to go into a fund for buying foot-salve, new clothes and children's toys for the marchers.

As a student I was appointed a kind of tally-clerk by Uncle Edwin.

I accepted the fees and thanked the girls. The night was long, delirious, marked by a breaking down of barriers that drove ten policemen to drugs and confirmed Lady Astor in her first opinion of marching militants.

Two days later I arrived back at Oxford relaxed, confident and so overtly not caring a damn that no one bothered to ask where I'd been. I discovered later that no one knew I had gone.

Into The Sunrise

For me, from childood, the name and fact of Russia have been loud on the wind. In my valley, the militants peered into every corner, looking for powers to subvert, pieties to thrash, blacklegs to harass, bailiffs to outrage, orthodoxy to knock, and usually finding them. Occasionally these subversive lads would be collared and whipped off to gaol. We took an operatic joy in their martyrdom.

In packed public meetings we groaned with sympathy whenever an orator pointed his tongue at the judge who had put them inside and the turnkeys who kept them there. When they were released we awaited their homecoming on the town square. They would be significantly wan, a stone or so thinner after a few months of being off chips, good cheer and salutary agitation. We applauded them until hoarseness or the pitch dark intervened. The victims had their rewards. As true bullfighters of the dialectic they touched some nerve of sexual excitement and, like any Spanish torero, seemed to wear a tail of compliant girls. A more lavish accolade was a trip to Russia.

I have an impression of a whole stream of these lads trudging down the hill bearing old and fissile suitcases, on the first lap of a journey to Moscow, for ideological stiffening, or to the Crimea for an infusion of socialised sun and fun. It always surprised me to think that Yalta might coax a smile out of these frowning paladins, for they were an earnest crew.

When they returned they spoke copiously of the rough, muscled paradise coming swiftly to birth on the other side of the Baltic. One, I recall, brought back a fine line in sad, Ukrainian folk songs, which he sang in the chip-shop. It disgusted the chip merchant, a man marbled in ancient loyalties who was waiting for the Duke of Wellington to stop dallying in stupid death and come back to oust the local socialist MP. The rest of us, sensitive to sad songs, broad vowels and plangent sounds from distant places, shed exciting tears over our shared length of hake.

For the conformist and timid, this trickle of heretics into the Soviet Union took on the qualities of a sinister folk-tale, as if Russia were an unbreached medieval forest into which fair children were abducted and slain. If anyone were not seen around for several weeks, no one ever thought he might be fugitive from debt or boredom. He was in Minsk or Norovabad, wearing a commissar's badge, choking tractors, blaspheming and getting the Celt a bad name around Whitehall.

In my early twenties, savouring a post-graduate gloom in an emphatically pre-graduate world, I stood in a darkened convenience on Porth square. Some splenetic ratepayer had stoned the light-bulbs to discourage further investment in this kind of amenity. Two men came in. One of them was talking. Even outside that sounding crypt his voice would have been strikingly loud and dramatic.

I heard my name mentioned. "Do you know who he is?" The second man muttered that he did not know, did not care. He was in trouble with the shadows, groping his way towards his niche and occasionally going headlong over patches of loose floor material. The vandals had won a prize with that convenience.

The first man went on. "A scholar, a book reader. Gaunt bloke. Very stooped. Wild eyes. Wrote a pamphlet denouncing decency, tithes and the minister of Labour, Mr Ernest Brown, a man of God and a voice of thunder in the right shaped pulpit. A chronic denouncer, this Thomas. Do you know where he is now?"

The second man's hand had now landed with stunning force against the wall above his niche and he was caring even less. "He's in Moscow," said the first man, "being trained as a spy. So if you see him, when and if he comes back, don't go blurting out any secrets. Even if it's only about our Sunday School hiring a marquee at Barry this year for the tea. God knows what the Russians might make of that. All those Christians under one canvas roof. Happy, relaxed, replete, vulnerable. Keep it to yourself if that Thomas is about. Let him hear it and he'll be spying full pelt. He'll rig up his little wireless and that Stalin will be in the know by Thursday."

The second man, more confident now about the dark, said he would be vigilant. They shuffled out of the convenience. When I had recovered from the shock of discovering that I might be trained for anything, I followed them.

It was not until an epoch later that I clapped eyes on the Kremlin. By this time the name and fact of Russia had become less emotive, sang more quietly on the wind. The old hot ardours had cooled and greyed into clinker. The world had been savaged, concussed and had become quieter. The warriors of the Marxist word had slipped into apathy or the earth. Their voices were not heard save in some bit of sardonic late-night musing.

My own rancours had shrunk to an obsessional loathing of social columns and a manic brooding on how and why Morton's modest little Elizabethen Fork had become the multilateral fiscal scythe I had spent my life failing to dodge. One echo remained. He was a man called Ike, a long-distance dissident, and during the whole period of our being neighbours, ailing on a broad front. He was one of the people who had been dispatched to the Soviet Union in the early 'thirties for a bout of curative calm after having been in gaol for resisting evictions.

Ike and his brother also carried a small, illegal printing press about the town in a clothes basket, and on this press he would print notices about the date of the imminent rising of the breechless against the over-clothed. The few notices to roll from this press, a pre-Caxton job by all reports, were so dim and illegible it was thought likely that Ike's brochure of instructions had left out all reference to ink.

People who stepped briskly from the Bolshevik camp to the spiritualist (a curiously large number) tried in later years to contact Ike's posthumous self to ask him, out of simple curiosity, what date he had had in mind.

I got to know Ike well in his last years. Illness and penury had made a shabby cartoon of the lad he had been at the start of the journey. He sat woodenly on the knee of the petrifying past and muttered with ventriloquial sadness. He was being tormented by the flagging momentum of his blood and dreams. He was also being bullied out of life by his wife, a fractious, abusive and powerful woman, a sergeant-major of dour convention.

Occasionally Ike would point out to me the house in Penygraig where Trotsky, then a fleeting messenger of the Comintern, getting the Rhondda into marching order for the last advance on what Ike called "the Pyramids of the last Pharoahs", had stayed and eaten chips out of paper.

Ike never seemed to point to the same house twice and it was clear that his memories were failing in point and coherence. It turned out that the man who had stayed in Penygraig was not Trotsky at all but a person called Kautsky, an itinerant German jeweller, neat in his habits, non-political and averse to chips.

Ike also sang a Russian song. It was Ukrainian. He claimed to have learned it in a village where, briefly, he had known some beaker of special enchantment. The melody was vague. Every time he sang it his wife, in a voice of amplified thunder, told him to shut up. One sultry afternoon Ike did so, for good.

I was reminded of Ike on my first journey to the Soviet Union. I flew there in an Ilyushin jet. I expected the customary swift flow of drink that alone makes these experiences credible. In the first hour I got one boiled sweet. I doubted whether I could continue to live at this pace for the next two and a half hours. But at the first hour's end came food. My cutlery slid at once to the floor from my sloping table. I could do nothing about it. I never undo my seat belt once I have secured it. One day I will carry this phobia to a point where I will arrive at the hotel of my destination city dragging the plane behind me.

During the third hour vodka flowed like the Don but less quietly. My neighbour was a man who had left Russia as a boy and was returning after thirty-six years. He was eager to see a village in south west Russia whose name he could not at that moment recall. Some loving uncle had lived there. We kept pace in our drinking, bottle for bottle, laughing at the price every time we took a sip, like children at a newly discovered sea.

He began to cry. I began to sing to him the song that Ike had sung. Coming from me it sounded even vaguer than it had at the start. I asked him if he knew it. He could not place it. But it served to remind him, in some mysterious way, of the name of the village he wished to revisit.

And that, on an earth where the lost are a nation in themselves, is something.

A Wish To Know

Twenty of us could get comfortably into the snug of The Crossed Harps. Philosophically we were as fissile a group as ever raised their voices over beer. On topics like the emergent nations, promiscuity as a social tonic and the future of local branch lines we were split right down the middle.

That is why on Friday and Saturday nights we preferred, around about nine o'clock, to sing. We would start with 'Now is the Hour' which one of our number could sing in what he told us was Maori, and we ended with 'Goodnight, Ladies', sung very softly in deference to the landlady, Mrs Hopgood, whose headbones were just about to give up the ghost at this point of the week. We had two highlights: 'Passing By' and 'Now the Day is Over', the first with a solo part for tenor, the second with a solo for baritone, the rest of us coming in from behind with a boom of rich, humming harmonies.

We would have said that trouble could never come to a group so skilled in evading tension and dispute. But the clouds form and we are here to be rained on.

The first cloud was called Hesketh Snell. Hesketh was a good baritone and when he went off the rails the sound of it could be heard all over the zone. It is easy now to see the reasons for his falling apart as a social being. He was disappointed not to be asked to do the solo baritone part in 'Now the Day is Over'. His voice had too rough a maturity to bring out the childish overtones in this lyric. He also worked in a small factory that made glue from bones and let out a smell that darkened the grass and drove people to switch faith and even nationality. The neighbours for some reason seemed to blame the whole thing on Hesketh as if he were the first to spring glue on the world as a fact. They looked on him as if he were presenting his credentials as the envoy of a major lazaretto. This affected his style of singing, for in the middle of a significant phrase he would drop his head as if ardently conscious of the world's eyes and a township's curse. This muffled his tone.

Then he began suspecting his wife of extra-mural adventures, although everyone knew that the walls in Meadow Prospect were too short for effective expression in this field. But Hesketh had a friend, Leopold Laity, a fellow gleeman, with a reasonably good tenor voice especially in the higher, more spectral levels of the top register, but a man with a malignant view of life. Laity was always hissing into Hesketh's ear baleful analyses of current moral trends. He had convinced Hesketh that Mrs Snell was moving as fluently as Pompadour through the turbid pool of the town's vagrant amours. Laity also kept suggesting to Hesketh that the general hatred of the glue-smell was such that it was only a matter of months before Hesketh would be seized and boiled down with his last imported bone. We took Laity to one side and spoke to him as a gleeman. We told him to choose between harmony and malice. He managed to hang on with the gleemen while still contriving to discharge enough gossip to unsettle Hesketh. But the combination of all these forces deranged Hesketh. He felt the need for some gesture of arrogant defiance. He got hold of a small gun and committed a series of burglaries that showed neither subtlety or profit. He was caught and tried. The judge was sympathetic. We, as gleemen, gave the court a collective testimonial to the gentleness of Hesketh and our own disbelief that a male voice chorister could behave in this way. Hesketh was given a conditional discharge. His trouble, said the judge, was schizophrenia, a persistent shake in his mental tiles under too heavy a wind of suggestion. He told Hesketh to turn the key on Hyde and re-sign his contract with Jekyll.

But Hesketh went to it again. There is no fixative that will serve a man whose psyche is seriously bent on falling to bits. This time, in the course of breaking into a warehouse, he fired his gun and grazed the top of a night watchman's head.

He was caught again. The odds are that he might have got away had it not been for another gleeman, Dorian O'Moore. Dorian had come shooting out of a back lane at the same moment as Hesketh was haring away from the police down a main street. Hesketh crashed into Dorian and they were both so stunned the police kept them both in the station until the mists lifted.

Dorian's story was that he had been keeping a date with a woman of his acquaintance when he had been attacked by a lover or husband. But Leopold Laity convinced Hesketh not only that the lady in the back-lane was Hesketh's wife, but also that Dorian had launched himself like a torpedo deliberately to cut short Hesketh's flight. Dorian was so horrified by these accusations his voice lost half its force and he was excused duty in our vocal group except on such things as lullabies where huskiness is not a hindrance.

Hesketh was put away for a fair period in one of our more solemn gaols. Three months later he escaped. He did so with feats of tunnelling and scaling so prodigious and bold he won headlines in every paper in the land. We read of how Hesketh, using only mailbag needles as his digging tool, had made his way from his cell to an airshaft and used a length of steel scaffolding to pole-vault over the main wall. As we brooded over these details we grew to feel less trapped ourselves and several voters even asked where they could get hold of mail-bag needles to deal with states of blockage they were noticing in their lives. One of our gleemen, a governor of one of our Grammar Schools, withdrew his campaign to resist the introduction of pole-vaulting into the School Sports on the grounds that it would never serve a useful purpose.

Hesketh's father appeared on television and made a statement. "They call my son a gunman," he said. "He only had a small gun like this." And he held his four fingers apart at a distance that suggested that Hesketh's gun had been about one tenth of the size of a derringer.

The effect on Dorian O'Moore was ruinous. He was convinced that Hesketh had broken out of gaol to fix him for having floored him beneath the very boots of the law. We tried to assure him that Hesketh would not be such a fool as to head homeward. We had often heard Hesketh declare an interest in the Arctic circle, and even now, we told Dorian, he was probably fishing for cod under an assumed Finnish name off Reykjavik. Every time we put that point to Dorian, Leopold Laity, now riding a most masterly crest of mischief, would come rushing in with the evening paper which announced that Hesketh's tracks showed him to be coming nearer and nearer to Meadow Prospect.

The town itself was in a panic. Any shadowy figure was seized and questioned. Lovers declared a moratorium. Three times the police with speed and noise of television standard closed in on the same tramp, a man called Hotchkiss, an undecided element who covered very little ground. The police and the Rotary Club gave

Hotchkiss five pounds on the understanding that he would move forty miles to the west and thin out the confusion he caused by hanging about in the lane behind Hesketh's house.

Hesketh came back gently, harmlessly. When asked what had caused him to take all this trouble, he said he had thought a lot about the theme of pollution on this earth and the smell from the glue-factory, wondering whether the people had been justified in thinking so badly of him for being an agent of this nuisance. Standing in front of the glue-factory at night, made unbearably sensitive by weeks of hunger and flight, he had inhaled deeply and decided that he had deserved gaol if only for having had to do with this traffic in bones. He had thought also of Leopold Laity, that tenor Iago, and on his way from the factory to the police station for a rest and a meal had called in at Laity's and fetched him a clip that left Laity quiet and unmalicious. It was at least a fortnight before Laity started giving out vindictive bulletins on life again. We also gave him the tenor solo in 'Passing By' to see if it would sweeten his peculiar mixture.

The Comeback

In all the tormented annals of amateur music there can have been few things more fitful, more unchartable than the life of the Meadow Prospect Jubilee Band. Bouts of delirious artistry would be followed by moods of recession, and silence would form around the township like moss.

Most of the bandsmen seemed to be men of a fierce, Dionysian bent. After weeks of placidly blowing away in their Band House, they would go off and play an away date which would end in revels of disastrous scope. They would return to the stares of wives and pastors. The urge to make harmony would drop down dead. Instruments would be returned to the Band House and a sackful of mothballs would be placed around their uniforms of plum and gold. The moustache of their conductor, Mathew Sewell, normally a trim and gay article when the tide of assertion was running right, became slack and sullen.

This happened one spring, after a fierce winter that had fretted our collective wind-pipe. We were glad of the returning warmth but our joy was muted without the chance to march solemnly in step behind or alongside the flashy uniforms of the Jubilee boys.

This attracted the attention of Dr Mackworth, a genial healer of the period who had a fancy for tickling the town's artistic ribs every time he saw its face becoming intolerably blank. That spring, the blankness was total. Dr Mackworth described the place as being propped against a tomb.

He called in one night at the long room of 'The Nest,' a pub much used by the bandsmen. The doctor found a significant nucleus of band members present. There was Gomer Gough, who played a surprisingly gay flute for so ponderous a debater; Edwin Pugh, who blew a sad oboe that perfectly matched his face and thoughts. With them was Cynlais Coleman, a noisy voter who seemed to turn everything on earth into a drum. Coleman could never see two bits of metal, however separate, without wishing to bring them together with a bang. It was thought that making him a drummer and percussion expert in the Jubilee would localise and lessen his powers as a nuisance. There were disputes about this. They were sitting in silence looking at the moon that was giving a gloss of pagan interest to the hillside.

Dr Mackworth stood over them sipping a stout and looking admonitory.

"Get blowing and marching again. Your silence is giving the place a look of rust. You haven't played a note since that carolling tour on Christmas Eve ended on a note of orgy and a message of ex-communication from ten different sects. All right, you've had your purge of purdah. Now face the light."

Their only answer was to move their chairs a little closer to the great fall of moonglow outside.

"There are people you ought to be helping."

"Who now?" said Gomer Gough who, at whatever depth of apathy, wanted the human map of the meadow to be clear.

"Your euphonium player, Bleddyn Bibey the Blast, for a start."

Gogh, Pugh and Coleman looked as if whatever nerve of pity they might have felt for Bibey had been snipped years since.

"Bibey got married a month ago. He is now living in that little flat on the first floor of the Band House. Married that Ceridwen Dando. Interesting girl. Patient of mine. Courtly, but destitute. An itching combination. Wouldn't marry Bibey until she was sure he wouldn't lay a lip to the euphonium again. Thought of a man blowing into any kind of massive pipe puts her on edge. She can't sleep. She knows that at least one half of Bibey's small mind is still in the band room below, and his mouth still puckered in the act of union with his chosen instrument. If Ceridwen Dando's doubts about marriage were to be transported she'd need a train. If you started up the band again, it would give her neuroses a chance to come out fighting and be healed. And there's Geraldus Gadd."

"What about Gadd?"

"One of your best cornet players. Kicked out by his father, a pietist, after that Christmas orgy. In lodgings now. You know that he was courting that Ceridwen Dando at the same time as Bibey. As lovers, over-emphatic, and their mental state played hell with their fingering when playing the faster scores. He was thrown out of the band for exceeding the highest permitted number of false notes on the very day that Bibey won the hand of the girl Dando. Now he's staying in his bedroom, brooding himself into a decline."

The bandsmen looked as if this was just the place and programme for Gadd. But soon the moonlight and the doctor's thesis that life loves an occasional challenge brought them to heel. They left 'The Nest' and rallied as many of the bandsmen as they could. They went over to the Band House.

They let themselves in quietly, not wishing to disturb Bleddyn Bibey and his wife who had already gone to bed. They collected their instruments, producing a muted note or roll from them to make sure they still worked.

In the flat above, Mrs Bibey was in a mood of sour wakefulness. That night she and Bibey had had a loud row. Since, she had argued, the band was not likely to reform, she saw no reason why they, as virtual caretakers of the Band Room, should not sell the instruments. Before he would see that done, said Bibey, he would set the place alight and die like a viking on a bed of molten brass.

Then sitting upright alongside the prone and snoring Bibey, she began to hear stealthy movements below. No voices; just the movement of feet, then tootles, trills, hoots, booms and thumps on drums, all very hushed and ghostly. She leaned over to make sure that all these noises could not possibly be coming from Bibey. Then she fled down the backstairs to her parents' home determined to have the Band Room exorcised, her marriage annulled and Bibey gaoled.

Gomer Gough, as deputy conductor, led his bandsmen up to the high street where the failing cornettist, Geraldus Gadd, lived. They were playing a quick march that gave an elfin ripple to the moonlight. The older neighbours were alarmed when they heard that the bandsmen were out to revive and rescue Gadd from his mortal gloom. They liked Gadd the way he was, for, in his days of fitness, not only had Gadd been a tireless amorist but he had a way of laying down a preliminary barrage on the heart of the chosen one with his cornet, which he hardly ever played in tune when emotionally prowling.

Gadd's landlady refused them permission to enter. So the bandsmen stood around and played a waltz selection. The younger people came gliding out the side-streets dancing and touched by a smiling madness. Cynlais Coleman stood on a borrowed chair and beat a tattoo on Gadd's window.

Gadd opened his window. Coleman threw his cornet up to him. Gadd threw it back, and instantly, as if touched by some resurrective nostalgia, leaned out to grab it back. He dressed and came down. He joined the band and played with tremendous force and inaccuracy, leading the band in five involuntary seconds from the 'Merry Widow' waltz into the gallop from *William Tell*.

They took Gadd to a pub where he had three boiler-makers, a drink of whisky and beer designed by a local man in the desert fighting of the First World War to flatten the backs of camels. Gadd pointed to the town. "I will go down there. I will fix Sewell who accused me of having a pitchless tympanum. I will fix Bibey who stole my girl."

They followed him to the square on which the Band House stood. On the way there they saw Bibey's wife who was returning slowly to the Band House, persuaded by her parents that life in the main consists of things like getting used to euphonium players. Gadd broke into a run. Mrs Bibey broke into a faster run. She got the front door of the Band House closed behind her just as Bibey was sitting down to play an elegy on his euphonium. She embraced him and he slipped an octave from shock.

Outside, Gadd was playing some kind of war-song on his cornet, taking the instrument from his lips every whipstitch and calling on Bibey to come out and fight. Bibey came out, playing to the last stretch of his lung. His wife sheltered behind him, seeming to find a new security and delight in the great brazen authority of Bibey's playing. He and Gadd advanced towards each other, like classic gunfighters but with cornet and euphonium instead of guns.

When they got so near that they would have had to resort to something more decisive than music, up came Mathew Sewell, the band leader, at his most diplomatic. He listened for a moment to Gadd's playing, winced, muttered that he thought that what little had been left of Gadd's sense of pitch had blown away in the last gale. Then he shook Gadd by the hand and invited him back into the band as premier cornettist. Gadd proudly fell in with the other bandsmen and marched off to give a short concert on the town square.

Bibey was excused. He and his wife went back into the Band House and the moonlight was left in peace.

Ripe, I Cry

There were two large buildings on the southern bank of the River Moody in Meadow Prospect. One was a cinema, the Coliseum. The other was a jam factory. Neither building had any trace of beauty and both were owned by Luther Cann.

Luther was a small, flamboyant man. He always wore a bowler and a bow-tie which made him stick up like a flag-pole in a place where the majority of heads went in for flat caps and where concern for what went around the neck had reached its lowest ebb. Luther was a hedonist, apolitical and a loud foe of the dialectical ferment that went on in the Library and Institute. He said he made more sense out of the hissing that went on in the vats of boiling fruit in his factory. Whenever he was the chairman of a concert, which was often, for he was about the only person in Meadow Prospect who could say "Ladies and Gentlemen" in a suave, unthreatening way, he always remarked how grateful he was, how delighted to have become a purveyor at once of films and jam, unique dampers to slow the burning thoughtful discontent in the skull of man.

Often in the Col., when pacing up and down the aisle, followed by Charlie Lush, his chief usher, he would see some diehard dissident ignoring the screen and muttering things to his neighbours that put life in a bad light. Luther would send Charlie Lush to the factory and when he returned Luther would slip the dissident a threepenny pot of the sweetest product in Luther's catalogue.

Luther's ownership of both cinema and factory led to some brisk bits of barter. On Saturday afternoons Luther staged his children's matinee, "the rush," called that because between one and two p.m. on Saturdays the children swarmed down the hillsides like lemmings to crowd Luther's benches. When the benches were full Luther packed the side aisles and a fair number were pinned breathless to the wall, having the plot relayed to them by chains of interpreters who were out in the clear. The walls of the Col. were interesting. Luther was a Welsh patriot in his own style and he had the place festooned with murals suggesting the broad history of the Welsh Celt from the rout of the Iceni through a gallery of Welshmen who had helped to defeat Napoleon, and winding up with a portrait of the Conservative porter at Meadow Prospect station who had deliberately mislaid Lloyd George's gladstone bag in 1905. The murals did not last long. The Conservative porter was stealthily whitewashed by a group of Radicals in the course of a film whose musical efforts were loud enough to muffle the rustle of their brush work. A torrential type of condensation which on peak-nights gave the hall the feel of a poor bathyscope did for the rest. Clients shuffling too close to the wall could easily go home with a wheel of Boadicea's chariot. It was the one cinema you could enter without a stain on your character and leave with a portrait of General Picton on the back of your mac.

Admission cost one penny. If the economic curve was down, completely out of sight, or just twitching, we could raise this sum by taking two empty jampots along to Luther's factory and he would give us a penny for them. Then into the cinema, the penny still hot from Luther's grasp. A small group of entrepreneurs who had found an illegal way of entry into Luther's storage yard were too busy selling Luther's jampots back to him to have time for films. These boys slipped into adult vices five or six years ahead of the normal date.

Tickets were not issued. Charlie Lush, his eyes getting wilder as Luther, in apostolic vein, stood in the foyer demanding that none be turned away, cowered inside the door, the wire on which he speared the tickets on normal nights drooping at his side, to be used as a kind of dirk in the case of in-fighting which was often necessary, for baiting Lush was a noted local sport.

Luther liked to feel our attachment to him. He made a show of admitting us into the task of choosing the films we saw. He would appear on the stage, bowlered, smiling, urbane. "And next Saturday, children, I can offer you a choice between a film with Thomas Meighan and one with Tom Mix. I want the choice to be yours alone. Who's for Thomas Meighan?" We were delighted with the flavour of power this gave us. Every hand went up for Meighan. "Good. And who's for Tom Mix?" Every hand went up for Mix. We thought it treason not to vote for every motion put. "Right. Mix it is." Mix it always was. Luther seemed to have a tight line on every foot of film that Tom Mix ever made.

Once a year he gave us a special treat on the afternoon of Boxing Day. Entry was free and the film, personally chosen by Luther, was a special one. Usually it was a great spectacle. Rod la Roq in *The Ten Commandments* with Theodore Roberts immense as Moses. Emil Jannings in *Quo Vadis*, followed by a short talk from Luther urging us to remember what we had seen of Nero and lead decent lives. Hoot Gibson in *Flaming Frontiers* and various big Westerns with George O'Brien and Buck Jones, men whose breadth and gait we idolised. So many of us walked about with unnaturally extended chests and bowed legs, in tribute to O'Brien and Jones, that the medical officer diagnosed some new epidemic deformity and loaded the reservoir with calcium. Not only did we get into these shows for nothing, Luther also distributed gifts. Comics, nuts and oranges. Luther was friendly with a bookseller and a fruiterer whose lives were a stutter of trouble over such things as drink and venery, and they would periodically let Luther have their bankrupt stock. He also distributed pieces of folded paper which let out an explosive sound when sharply flipped. That gift was dropped when it was found to be dementing Charlie Lush who signalised the loosening of his last hinge by turning up for duty in a helmet of the First World War and his ticket-wire sharpened to bayonet sharpness. The quality of the fruit we got from Luther was poor. The oranges looked as if they had walked from Spain and the nuts had the name of a dentist stamped on the inner shell. But any hint of largesse in those days made a thunder of delight.

Then towards the middle '20s some part of the brightness went out of Luther. He himself had a lot of rheumatism brought on by standing between clients and the walls to defend his murals. Jam was selling on a market that had no place for sweetness. Many cinema customers were weaned away by the town's Band of Hope which had secularised its programme in a bid to win the gaiety stakes. Luther walked at the centre of a great pallor. Even his taste in films changed. He made a point of tracking down the most brooding, sentimental films. He sent a wire to Hollywood asking them to let him have a private copy of any picture they thought too depressing for general circulation. He showed a clutch of tearjerkers that promoted more grief than regret and remembrance. The clients were wetter than the walls. Then Charlie Lush became more recessive and this was considered a feat of movement, for no one in Meadow Prospect had ever seemed to be more pinned to the rockface than Lush.

On the Boxing Day of the year in which this decline began he threw his cinema open for the free film and the handing out of gifts. The gifts had come in for the plague of sadness. The comics all had a covert religious message; the oranges looked as if they were asking for political asylum and the nuts said quietly that they would need to be opened by gunfire.

The special film was *Over The Hill*, a film which, emotionally, burst over the Western world like a monsoon. The star was Mary Carr, an elderly actress who went through the cinema of the '20s having no luck at all. (In *The Ten Commandments* she was buried under a cathedral built by her son, Rod la Roq, a building contractor with less conscience than one of his winches. The son's mistress Vita Naldi, gets leprosy, a touch that had the deacons calling. They were given complimentary tickets by Luther who felt in need of a cheer from the theological rank after the local pietists had tabled a successful motion against jam as an immoral substance.) In *Over The Hill* Mary Carr was an old mother who gets put in the work-house by an ungrateful son. There is a loving son who is railroaded to gaol by the ingrate. When he is released he goes up the hill to the workhouse and fetches his mother down. The ingrate is struck by lightning. The audience were moved to a fury of desolation, weeping and sobbing at the volume of first-class wake, leaving the cinema thinking a lot better of mothers and lightning.

Before the film started Luther came on to the stage and said he hoped the film would move us to tears and pity. He saw the need for these things and he said he hoped to see us soaked and rueful when the lights went up.

The film began. It was sad as an old-fashioned walking funeral. Most of the children became distracted. There were shouted demands for Hoot Gibson, Douglas Fairbanks, Elmos Lincoln and the other vaulting extroverts of the period. Some of us in the gallery dropped our oranges and nuts on Luther and Lush as they moved up and down the aisles urging silence and compassion. That year most of us had been given flashlights, electric torches, for Christmas and we brought all these into play at once. The hall was lighter than day and only a few voters in the front benches, who were there by virtue of a special sort of myopia, could see what was happening to

Mary Carr. It was the first X-ray the Col. had ever had. The results were alarming. Luther and Lush were enveloped in a vast spotlight that made them look like emerging clowns. This upset Lush who had spent so many years in the darkness of the Col. he was more sensitive to light than a moth.

After half an hour of this Luther stopped the film. He told us he was disgusted, that if we were anything to go by the world was in for an eclipse of sympathy and that never again would there be a free Boxing Day matinee, never again a distribution of gifts.

Eleven months later Luther closed the Col. and sold the jam factory. He went to live in a small mansion surrounded by trees in the middle of the town and was never to be seen. His only link with the outside world was Charlie Lush whom he employed as valet and companion. It was a poor link, for Lush, as a communicant, was a faulty wire.

On Christmas Eve my mother paused in her mountainous task of baking and said it was a pity that this Boxing Day there would be no cinema treat. We agreed. Treats were thin on the tree. Then my mother said it would be a good idea if we went around and gave Luther a carol. We did not agree. A few nights before some friends of ours had gone up Luther's drive to do some carolling. They stood in the porch and started 'God Rest Ye Merry, Gentlemen.' Between verses they heard a kind of dry laughter from behind the door but they had paid no heed to this, thinking that the people inside were seeing more in this carol than they, being young, had been able to see. Then Luther and Lush, bearing what our friends said were weapons of pike and stave kind, had driven them down the drive setting the teeth of the Christian world decisively on edge.

The following day, Christmas morning, we thought again of what our mother had said. We relented. We went along to Luther's. We stood on the porch. We went through the whole range of carols. We listened carefully between items. There was no sound of dry laughing. We assumed that daylight had softened Luther's mood. Then he burst forth alone. We took it that Lush was inside priming the cannon. We did not pause to wonder. Luther chased us right around Meadow Prospect. We darted in through our kitchen door a mere yard ahead of his yearning boot. We slammed the door. He stood outside, ashen, panting and utterly sad.

Our Christmas dinner was being served. The kitchen was bulging with famished diners. My mother had invited every waif in the block and in addition to our own brood they made a small army. To have blunted our collective appetite we would have needed a turkey the size of a condor. Outside, Luther turned away, his shoulders in their black serge drooping like the flags of a last, dark surrender. My mother rushed out, brought him into the kitchen, set him down at the table. There were loud objections from the waifs and ourselves who thought that goodness had already been carried far beyond the bend of sense. Luther ate little. We saw to that. We had arranged ourselves so that he could barely raise his arms. But there were beginnings of a mild gladness on his face.

The following day, Boxing Day, he appeared at our door again, with Charlie Lush. We told him there was no food. We had vultured our way back to a total bareness. He said he did not want food. All he wanted was that we should gather the children of the hillside together.

Five minutes of running and whooping had the tribe assembled. Luther and Charlie led us down the hill. They opened the Col. Luther located the stationer and fruiterer in a nearby pub. Comics and fruit, rumpled and stale after the Christmas recess, were produced. The cinema was arctically cold. The special film was Douglas Fairbanks in *Robin Hood*. Luther, from the stage, made a statement in favour of outlawry and wassail. We grew so numb we peeled the comics and read the jaffas. Our sinuses thickened into a sullen catarrh that lasted well into the Spring. But it got the Col. opened again and Luther back to form. A point had been made.

After You With The Illusion

If you have a myth, hang on to it. Do not slip it off the leash and let it wander around.

For years I was perfectly happy as a promoter of mystique behind the international rugby matches held at the Cardiff Arms Park. Privately I had regarded them as the greatest acts of mental lapse since the launching of hashish and jazz but I never said so. I just helped build the myth. I lent my tongue in that cause to some of the most alarming nonsense since Nietzsche. "Nothing is more im- pressive than this outpouring of zealots in a thousand trains from all the valleys to the north. The molten life of our ancient tribes flows south as if at the call of Owen Glyndwr making his promised return from his sleep among the grey rocks." If Glyndwr took one look at the sixty thousand rain-driven shamans roaring and gaping behind their monstrous rosettes at the Arms Park he would go back at the double and tell those grey rocks that this time it was for keeps.

Or, another line: "You have not stood at the fervent core of the real Welsh heart until you have taken your place in a capacity crowd at the Arms Park to sing the Welsh national anthem." Try standing there. If this is the Welsh heart the valves are really jumping. The band, a brisk lot nourished on Sousa and marching behind goats, is never fewer than three bars ahead of the herd. The singers them- selves, when not worrying about what hybrid chant will emerge from that racket to do service for the anthem written by the James boys of Pontypridd, are all trying to harmonize with the echo that is coming three seconds late from the corners of the vast stand.

Anyway I was caught out. Willie Silcox the Psyche told me at Tasso's Coffee Tavern that my material about the great Welsh myths was getting a bit thin; so I should go to one of these sporting events. I told Silcox that prophets could surely dispense with actuality. Had Taliesin, I asked, been present at those battles from which he had wrung such first-rate woe? Silcox was sure he had and he had already fished out a reference to Taliesin running like a hare in some retreat from the North Midlands and composing easily on the hoof. Even so, I said, I hated crowds. I cited an uncle who had been caught in a swirling mob at Birchtown and had spent hours in our kitchen showing off the toothprints in his body and even identifying people from them. Silcox was certain that the Arms Park had a system of ingenious concrete boxes into which groups of about thirty people were shepherded to watch the game in safety.

We agreed to go, and to take with us my neighbours Edwin Pugh the Pang and Teilo Dew the Doom, who have grown no happier since they have been attending that adult-education class on the world's shrinking food supplies. I agreed with Silcox that exposure to some sort of gladiatorial clash would help give these two voters a cooler view of man's threatening mouth.

Silcox got the tickets. We went to Tasso's on the Friday night to pick them up. We found Tasso standing behind his tea-urn and peeping out without love or confidence at two elements who were sitting in the shop with Silcox. Both were men noted even in Meadow Prospect, a compost heap of neuroses, for taking a nervous view of life. One, Nathan Hughes, was fitting his mouth around a long, trumpet-like instrument. With one blow in ten he would get a note out of this contrivance which drove a score of people away from Tasso's as their fingers touched the latch. The other voter, Goronwy Heppenstall, had in his hand a huge bell which he shook every time Nathan's instrument came to life.

"This is the way out for these boys," said Silcox. "Nathan and Goronwy have heard articles like these, the Alpine horn and the cowbell, being used on the radio at soccer internationals and they are going to use them at Cardiff tomorrow. It will give them a new confidence. It will also remind them of the healing tranquillity of the Alps."

"Unhappiness in Lombardy," said Edwin Pugh, "first drove Tasso up here to Meadow Prospect. After years of study Silcox has found the combination that will drive him back there."

The following morning we called for Teilo Dew. There was the sound of hammering from a shed in the back. Some neighbours had gathered around the shed, having heard Teilo say more than once that his great wish was to fashion a definitive coffin for the hopes of mankind. Mrs Dew, from the kitchen, told us that she could not be sure that Teilo was on this tack, but only the night before she had been put off her cheese and onion supper by a long talk from Teilo on why a desperate nihilism might not yet be a better bet than the Band of Hope.

Teilo came out of the shed looking quite cheerful. He was carrying a roughly shaped box, quite large but certainly no coffin.

"I can't stand on concrete," he said. "My sinuses stand up and sing at any hint of cold concrete. So I will stand on that box and be comfortable."

"That's a pretty tall box," said Edwin, "and these football crowds are fierce. If they can't see with you on that box you'll finish up in it."

"Oh, they'll understand," said Teilo, and the neighbours were surprised and pleased by his simple confidence.

On our way to the station we were joined by Nathan Hughes and Goronwy Heppenstall, carrying the Alpine horn and cowbell and putting up with a lot of gibes and catcalls from some elements in woollen caps. One of them was imitating a cow. I recognized him as a boy with a long record for roaming about the streets of Meadow Prospect on a Saturday morning wearing a massive Balaclava helmet and maddening the voters with insolent bits of mimicry. Nathan Hughes had his horn held above his head like a club and looking tormented. We tried to hurry our steps, but Willie Silcox came hurrying out of a shop and said he wanted us to see Nathan and Goronwy safely to Cardiff.

"They're a bit shy," he said, "and if they try to hide those fine extrovert contraptions, keep them at it."

We went into the station. The train was packed when it came in. When the people in the compartments saw us, Hughes with his horn, Heppenstall with his cowbell and Dew with his box held stiffly in front of him, they told Redvers Hallett the guard that they would get out and do something to the station and the track if he did not put us five safely in the van at the end of the train. So we were put in there, with some dogs, pigeons and budgerigars. Hallett had a budgerigar in a cage at his side and it was clear from the way he looked at this bird that it meant something special to him. He was so absorbed he did not even ask us why Heppenstall and Hughes should be lugging such unWelsh instruments into Cardiff. Hallett told us about the budgerigar. Its name was Ewart. He had taught it to recite whole passages from the speeches of well-known libertarians, urging men and women to cast off their shackles. The budgerigar could not be made to shut up, and Hallett's wife had to bear the brunt of it. After listening to Ewart the budgie speak quite clearly on the degradation of women she ran off with an insurance agent and an endowment of Hallett's which had just ripened.

"Since she left, Ewart hasn't spoken a word," said Hallett, and we all said how sorry we were to hear of this whirl of deprivations that had struck Hallett. Edwin tried mentioning the names of some famous Radicals to the budgerigar and kept saying "Come on, Ewart, let's have you," but Ewart just stayed dumb in the corner of its cage, staring at Hughes and Heppenstall as if it understood exactly how they felt.

"I'm coming off duty when we reach Cardiff and I'm taking Ewart to a cousin of mine who keeps a pub there. They say the smell of drink brings a budgie's vocal urge to the peak. Besides I hate my cousin. He's a great traditionalist and when he hears the subversive chatter that comes from Ewart he's going to be upset."

At Cardiff an immense crowd was pouring down a narrow street to the ground. When they saw us approach, Hallett in the lead with his bird cage, they opened ranks to let us pass, glad that the Celts in their flight from funerals as a way of life seemed now with our tableau to have completed the trip. Nathan and Goronwy said they would need a few pints to work up the sort of blithe expression they had seen on the faces of the hornblowers and cowbell ringers shown on the television.

Hallett took us to his cousin's pub. It was a tumbledown little place in which the dart board seemed to be the only clean and stable thing. All around us patriotism and benevolence had flowed in with the fourth and fifth pint. Some people, seeing Teilo's box followed by Nathan and Goronwy looking so sad and tense with those instruments, thought they were needy buskers and told Teilo to keep his box the right side up if he wanted a Christian response from the drinkers. We found ourselves pinned in a corner with a short mad man who had been present at every international match played at Cardiff since 1905. He explained why he had disagreed with every decision ever made by the referees at these events. He was enraged and almost killed Teilo Dew with his glass when Dew suggested that he had probably got hold of some false rule book devised by some droll squire who was out to twit the Celts for their devotion to the handling code. Edwin Pugh quietened the man by quoting to him a poem by Housman and that Methodist hymn which says just about the last word on transience and death, even among referees. I fingered the clapper of Heppenstall's cowbell and pulled it gently from time to time to throw in a graveyard overtone.

At three the pub emptied and Hallett's cousin took us into the kitchen at the back. There we had barley wine and cockles and we all looked at each other with a fine sensual glow. Hallet's cousin wept a little when he heard the story about Hallett's wife and the insurance man because he himself was very drunk by now and had been prone to disaster in his own love life. But Hallett was laughing and praising insurance. We heard the Welsh anthem being sung from the rugby ground. We all stood up, stiff as ramrods. Heppenstall and Hughes did what they could by way of accompaniment and Teilo Dew beat on his box to suggest a drum. Even Ewart the budgie got up from its corner and stood on a perch but no sound came from it. Then Edwin Pugh got sad and started making a symbol of the budgie in whose throat the wild words of golden affirmation had died. The cloak of banality falls, said Edwin, and the glorious dreams of a laundered species shuffle off into a shabby gloom. I could see that Edwin had Hallett's cousin foxed and uneasy and he had paused and shaken his head once or twice on his way to get fresh supplies of the barley wine and cockles. I nudged Edwin and asked him why we should spoil a good thing. Every few minutes the crowd in the ground roared and we stood up and roared with it.

The crowd had been streaming away from the ground for half an hour when we left the pub. As we stood at the door of the kitchen Ewart the budgie came to life and made one of the clearest statements I have ever heard from bird to man. It was a vigorous paragraph from a speech by Henry Richards made in 1870 explaining why drink for the next two hundred years will continue to rob the working man of his full dignity. Hallett's cousin had his ear in the cage, not missing a word.

It was a good session. Now all we have to do is think up a story to tell Silcox about the match itself.

No Dancing On The Nerve-Ends, Please

One night at Tasso's Coffee Tavern I saw Willie Silcox take time off from an angry speech he was making to the wall. A few minutes before, Milton Nicholas and Cynlais Coleman had been between Silcox and the wall and had given a sane look to the address but they had now moved off and were standing by the counter being shown views of Naples by Tasso. In between pictures Milton muttered to Silcox to drop his voice if he was going to keep on talking in an apparent vacuum.

So Silcox fell silent and came over to the counter and pretended to be impressed but he annoyed Tasso by saying that he thought some of the voters pictured in the cards looked very primitive and could do with jacking up to a higher level of awareness. He even slipped a few progressive pamphlets out of his pocket, one on rate-differentials in Meadow Prospect, another on segregation in South Africa. Tasso pushed the pamphlets back, with a free coffee for Silcox to blunt the blow, and said that the Neapolitans were in enough of a fog now, between too much singing, many invasions, an excessive natural jocosity and an arbitrary-minded executive.

That set Silcox off again.

"If Naples," he said, "has got a worse policeman than that Leyshon the Law who casts the shadow of his baton over Windy Way then God help them down there in that sunlit bay of which you have been showing us such fine views."

"What has he been doing, the Leyshon?" asked Tasso. Milton and Cynlais groaned and asked Tasso for the dominoes. They had heard the story before.

Silcox was in the Institute Amateur Drama group and they had entered a regional knock-out competition. Their rivals were a company to which Leyshon the Law belonged. Silcox's group were putting on what he called a hard-hitting drama on the dangers of a trouble to the flesh called 'the Spanish evil' in the play, written at a time when about the only answer to this ailment was prayer. Silcox played the respectable head of a family in France who finds himself hemmed in by this murrain. His father had it and he has passed it on to his son. And all this in mockery of the fact that he himself has lived his whole life on a glacier of pious restraint that had amazed most of the other Frenchmen and damaged the tourist trade. When time and caution had thinned the plague a stray would come along into the family's ranks and invigorate the virus; the virus in this case was Silcox's wife, a mezzo-soprano called Jacqueline Hacket and the best exponent of the off-white on the Meadow Prospect stage. Silcox caused a lot of nervousness with some of his speeches. The real evil of evil, he said, was its cunning obliquity. Wrap yourself around with as many layers as you liked of black, forbidding serge and chilly texts, your defences would be of no avail. The transmitted venoms of peccant forebears would still strike to the heart and make of you their crumbling and helpless clown. Some of the audience who had been bolstered for decades on serge and texts offered Silcox the freeplaying rights of 'Charley's Aunt' to get him off this line. But Silcox was delighted with it. The son was played by a young man called Arfon Gaxton, well-known for his look of terror even when he was not on the stage with Silcox pointing out the way to the clinic and the grave.

When Silcox's group were rehearsing the play for the final elimi-nating bout with Leyshon's players, Arfon was in some trouble. He had been sitting at the back of our local cinema, the Coliseum, with his girl, oblivious of the film and with his emotions on the draw, largely as a kind of escape from the shadow of Silcox and those terrible warnings. The lights of the cinema had gone on in the middle of a film without any hint on the part of the ushers. The manager, Luther Cann the Col, marched on to the stage to make a short speech. Cann was always doing this. He would be sitting in his tiny box office getting anxious about his patrons and then he would switch the lights on unexpectedly and come on to the stage to make a speech in which he would urge the voters to be silent, brighter or just clean, depending on the current of Cann's phobias on the night. Arfon Caxton had been slow to act after Cann's fingers touched the switches and he had been caught in what Leyshon the

Law later described, going on notes furnished by Cann, as "a shocking posture". We tried to press Leyshon to a fuller definition but all he did was shake his head and say that from now on we could forget Nero and that the goats would turn around when Arfon Caxton passed.

 We called in to see Luther Cann to ask him not to press charges and Silcox explained to Luther, speaking very slowly, that we had to be tolerant in this case because a frank hedonism and a pagan flourish were things you had to expect from a born actor. I think that speech moved the last stone into position for Arfon Caxton. There is always a jaunty excess of pressure about Silcox's style that brings out the strongest Calvinistic juices in Luther Cann. He took Silcox as hinting that in the cause of bringing Caxton's talent as an actor to full flower he should suspend films and hand over the back row permanently to Caxton and license. Luther hurried to turn over the facts to Leyshon the Law and on the very night of the show, when Arfon was on the stage, going half-mad under the strain of having Silcox tell him of the medical doom that is following him around like a scurvy dog, Leyshon, in full uniform, appeared in the wings and held his hands out towards Arfon in the suggestion of handcuffs. He also waved a summons that told Arfon that the game was up and that he would soon be explaining his conduct to that most Mosaic of magistrates, Elfed Fraser the Frown.

"Can you imagine the effect of that on a type like Arfon Caxton?" Willie Silcox asked Tasso. "With me standing there, as I do during my big speech, my arms over my head, my hair up on end and my eyes the size of that urn, telling Caxton that his teeth are shortly going to be put on edge by a family line of sleepless lechers and debauchees, this silver-buttoned janissary, Leyshon, comes creeping into the wings to tip Caxton the black spot." Leyshon's play won the contest as you probably know. Leyshon himself, in this play, is an ape who looks like a man, and he is slipped off the leash every whipstitch by some voter who is out for the world power and if anybody stands in this voter's way Leyshon, the man-ape, strangles them or pushes them through a window. If Leyshon had been given any lines to speak in this part you might say the part was written for him. But as it is he just has to go about as an ape, and illiterate for that reason.

Silcox fished a paper from his pocket. He searched through it for an item and showed it to Tasso.

"Look at that," he said. "'Drama Cup goes to Meadow Prospect'. But not for the fine, thoughtful drama we put on about the social implications of depravity and lust which did more to girdle the gonads than four chapels going all out. Oh no! It went to Leyshon's group, and just read out to these voters what it says there about Leyshon."

Tasso looked apologetic as if hinting that Silcox could read it out far better than he.

"'The performance of Police Constable Leyshon,'" he read, "'was praised by the adjudicators as a masterpiece of quiet naturalism. The Chief Inspector of the County Constabulary who presented the cup to the Gallileo Players said P.C. Leyshon was a credit to the force and a living testimony that brawn no longer ranks above brain in this branch of public service.'"

"'A masterpiece of quiet naturalism'," said Silcox and he gave a snort that made Cynlais duck. "Quite! He just shuffles about the stage and he doesn't say a word because he's an ape, just looking and shuffling like he's looked and shuffled about Meadow Prospect for years and this jay in the paper singles him out as a new Emil Jannings."

"And the Arfon Caxton?" said Tasso, wishing that Silcox would now calm down and create a proper atmosphere for the brisk coffee trade that normally set in about this time of evening. "The Arfon is no doubt by this time in the County Keep." "Thankfully no," said Silcox. "And we can thank Luther Cann and his brittle psyche for that. After those lights went on and Arfon Caxton was exposed in whatever posture it was that so shocked that prurient daub, Cann, Cann has taken to standing in the aisles just staring at the back row, alert for any sign of looseness. Cann has been in a very distraught state lately. He lost the skittles tournament in the Constitutional Club and, just after that, a young usherette caught him a hard one with her torch when Cann was bending over her in the shadows on some bit of supervision or other. So Cann has rubbed the censorious side of his mind into a state of rare rawness. Just a slight movement of the hand in that back row and Cann throws two torches into action, standing there with his arms thrown forward like an old-fashioned gunfighter. He shocked the wits out of a few elderly and blameless couples who accused Cann of adding a new and terrible dimension of disquiet to darkness and they were prepared to swear in court that Cann, as a spotter of sexual activity, was deranged. So

Arfon was discharged. What we need about here now, Tasso, is an altogether blander and more humane sort of policeman."

We put that notion into a formal recommendation which we sent by post to the Chief Inspector of Police. We have had no reply. Silcox thinks that Leyshon the Law might well have intercepted the letter. We'll never find out from Leyshon. Since that bit in the paper describing him as the new Jannings we haven't been able to get him to look at us.

The Little Baron

A t the summer's end Grospoint Castle became empty and passed into the hands of the local authority. The castle was a Norman foundation and the Grospoint family had been steadily in the residence since they had dangled some Celtic prince from the first rough keep in 1207. When they found their chain-mail getting heavy they slipped into the enclosure system, and by the time steam-power came they were gathering royalties on the slower breezes. Then taxes became brutal and they began to find it as dear to die as most of their tenants had found it to live. So they handed the fortress over to the local authority. The authority, with a puzzled look on its face, took it and said it might become a folk museum when the money situation eased.

I was asked to think of a temporary caretaker for the place. I thought instantly of Mungo Young, a harassed man who had been driven to the edge of madness by youths whom he had tried to restrain from playing the fool in the public park where he worked as a keeper.

The huge key to the front gate was handed over to Mungo. I and my friend Mansel Trask, who collects rates for the council, accompanied Mungo on his first morning of duty.

As Mungo trembled over the job of fitting the key, which he had been holding in front of him like a mace, into the keyhole, Mansel Trask, who like Mungo wore his nerves in the most fashionable loops, stared down into the moat which we had crossed by way of an ancient, worm-eaten bridge. "Here," said Mansel, "is a striking tableau. A son of the common people lets himself into this strong–hold with a key. In centuries past this moat was filled to the lip with the bodies of hillmen who had stormed its walls in vain." Mansel gave Mungo's arm a jerk that made him miss the keyhole by a foot. "You will find the place full of ghosts. With a sympathetic nature

like yours, Mungo, they will approach you boldly. Listen to them."
Mansel raised the brochure on the castle from which he had been
feeding facts to Mungo all the morning. "I can see you furnish- ing
a very useful appendix to this booklet, if you keep your senses
porous, on the hidden life of this pile." Mungo got the key into the
hole and muttered to me that if Trask was going to go on in that
strain he wished he were back in the park.

We helped Mungo get the door open. It gave out a sudden angry
whine and a wave of pigeons stirred up from the lovely lawns that
led up to the keep. Mungo, thinking he had run into the first line of
the phantoms mentioned by Trask, closed the door. I told Trask to
keep his remarks to Mungo on a more wholesome plane and pushed
Mungo forward.

During the week that followed we made a point of calling in at
the castle as often as we could in case Mungo should yield too much
to loneliness. The council had provided him, by way of uniform,
with a long, chrome-buttoned jacket, and had partly furnished the
porter's lodge for his accommodation. The lodge was four or five
times the size of the house Mungo had left. That dwelling had been
so small the mice had to hunch their shoulders if they wanted any
sort of independence. We noticed that Mungo was standing much
more erect, as if he wanted to keep every one of the chrome buttons
on full view.

Even about the lodge there were some rare ducal touches; one
painted ceiling and several scrolls of relief on the walls, put there,
according to Trask's handbook, to help a drunken porter of the
eighteenth century. He diluted his delirium in the ceiling and the
scrolls were phrases of gross abuse in Norman French which he
shouted at visitors through a little grille.

We shook Mungo by the hand to compliment him on his dignified
appearance. He seemed to take the tribute as his due. He told Trask,
who has a habit of bending low over the person he is talking to, not
to breathe on his chrome buttons. "In a place like this, they've got to
shine."

We inspected the rest of the place. Next to the porter's lodge was
a rough door that opened on to a deep hole. I was telling Mungo he
would have a job lugging coal out of this cavern when Trask found
in the handbook that this was a dungeon in which a nephew of
William Rufus, seized by the Grospoint of the day, had been kept
for eighteen years to go blind and die. "Thank God we've outgrown

that sort of thing," said Trask, but in his eye I could see the thought that for some of the more laggard ratepayers (for whose doors he had worked out whole tattoos of brusque and angry knocks) this hole which had been home for the nephew of Rufus, would, made deeper and a little darker, be just the place.

From there we went on to the ducal apartments. We went into a bathroom with the biggest bath we had ever seen. One duke of long ago had a way of diving into this tank and operating as a kind of sportive submarine. Trask was going to say that he thought this quite sensible when his eye dropped to a footnote which said that the duke often had his favourite girls stationed at various points of the bath as marker-buoys for these underwater jaunts. The duke drowned in his sixtieth year, laughing. Trask, a man wary to the point of death in matters of the flesh, almost blinked his lashes off when he read this, and Mungo had to grab him by the back of his blazer to prevent him reeling down a flight of forty stone steps.

We saw rooms ringed with bronze tigers, part of the family's armorial crest, and these tigers had originally had eyes of precious stones but these stones had now been removed and all that showed in the plundered sockets was a dark disgust. We saw the library in which, said Trask's handbook, "ten thousand volumes in bindings laced with gold leaf had glowed like the core of a sunset when the sun struck through the huge windows". The books had gone. The room seemed dun and cheated. The sun appeared to be looking for something. Only Mungo, in all that gutted apartment, was utterly satisfied. He made, in a low, rather severe voice, a late rider to Trask's remarks about the duke who had built his life around the bath: "If a duke, of all people, wants to look for the soap, he can, that's what I say." His tone made it clear that Mungo was speaking for the Grospoints, and Trask, rubbed into a rapture of suggestibility by all the stories of ruin and woe he had to hear from rates debtors, almost made a curtsey.

Then we went into the dining room. This room was decorated with mural paintings of incidents selected from the castle's early history. I noticed that many of the faces in these pictures had no eyes, just holes, and we found from the brochure that one of the Renaissance Grospoints had gone on a sort of Rhodes Scholarship to study with the Borgias in Italy. He had spent most of his evenings in late middle age stalking on a platform behind these murals, peering in through these holes at the guest to whom he had already served the dose and who would not last the meal.

Mungo, wearing a sly, disquieting smile, insisted that we find the small door that led to this platform, and he got us to sit down at the long table while he moved from head to head in the murals staring at us and occasionally shouting that he had got us under his eye and the mixture prepared. Trask and I agreed that next to having lived through a fundamentally violent epoch, with Trask's assorted traumas thrown in to thicken the mixture, this was about the most disturbing sensation we had ever known. When Mungo came out from behind the paintings he looked at us coldly as if surprised to find us still breathing.

Two days later we called to see him again. The great door was locked and did not open to our shouts. We saw Mungo glaring down at us from an embrasure as if awaiting his last order of hot lead when we shouted up to him to come out of the fortress while he was still somewhere near the mental hinge, he slipped down to the lodge and gave us a selection of those Norman French phrases of gross abuse through the grille.

The next day events short-circuited Mungo back to the track of truth. A cousin of Rhodri Todd, the mayor, a lady from America, very haughty, very rich, wanted to look round the castle. Rhodri Todd brought his cousin around himself. He was in the outskirts of a fit when he saw Mungo leaning on the parapets staring down at them as if they were beggars at the gate. He happened to know Mungo's social insurance number and shouted it up to him and reminded him that a job is a job, and that the relationship between master and man is still basically sharp-edged. That cut through the fog of centuries and brought Mungo, walking slowly, to the gate. He escorted the American lady round the castle. She expressed no pleasure, no interest. She listened with a deepening tedium to the mumbling extracts from the brochure that Mungo had committed to heart and recited like a life story. As we reached the bottom of the last flight of stairs he stopped, turned and asked her with a most seignorial air: "And what did madame think of that?"

"I have seen," she said, "all the chateaux of the Loire, all the schlossen of the Rhine, and for sheer knuckle-headed ostentatious vulgarity this really takes the belt."

"I knew you'd like it," said Mungo. Then he heard the loud, cruel laughter of Rhodri Todd and did the slowest double-take in the annals of slow understanding. He slapped the lady hard across the face and shaped up to Todd for a longer engagement.

It took Todd just an hour to have the chrome-buttoned jacket off Mungo and Mungo out of the castle. His barony had lasted for ten days.

Cover My Flank

Yesterday I saw Cyril Gill. His eyes were swollen. He had one arm in a high sling and he was limping. I thought the sling was unnaturally high, but that was his way. If he has anything, he'll show it to you. He did not beckon or nod at me as he passed. His brows were down as far as they would go and his face seemed to be slipping past even the accepted Meadow Prospect level for expressed melancholy.

Normally I do not like to see anyone walking along with a frown or a fracture, but in the case of Cyril Gill I relax the rules, for if anyone, over the years, has been down on his knees in front of life begging for a comprehensive clouting, it is Cyril. In a more naive, attentive day, he could have been important, a leader, the dispenser of a loud revelation. He gets flashes inside the mind which convince him that he has supernormal resources of knowledge and power. In a time and place quaking with silence, solitude, and dread, Cyril could have been another Moses. But in the Meadow Prospect of this decade he is simply a nuisance, and the local Council have played with a tentative by-law which would cause him to be flanked always by two friends whose duty it would be to tell him to stop being brilliant and authoritative in fields to which he has no passport.

We would not have minded if Cyril had used a cross-section of the town for his targets. But he seemed to single out one man as the proving ground of his inspirations. This was Ednyfed Beaumont. Ednyfed was a big man, strong as an ox and suggestible as a child. He was the rabbit to Cyril's stoat. Cyril had only to open his mouth and Ednyfed blinked.

One evening we were in the public bar of a pub called The Ingle. With us were Cyril and Ednyfed. The landlord of the pub, Derwent Stamp, was new to the business and very unsure of himself. That was why we wished to give him our support, although I would have preferred not to have Cyril with us. He was a djinn. On the counter was a colossal stack of pennies, piled carefully into a monolith by the customers and dedicated to a charity. The pile had grown beyond the limits of convenience. Derwent Stamp had failed to contact the organiser of the charity, who was supposed to come and cart the money away. He was nervous about it and was very glad that most of his customers were short and unable to place any more pennies on the top. But the charity had won support after the organiser, standing on a chair, had addressed the bar and got the pile started. So when anyone tall came in, he was normally handed a few pennies to add to the handsome column. Derwent spent most of his time telling people not to stand at that point of the counter. "If anyone's elbow touches that lot," he said, "there'll be another Gaza." He had once been on a nationally known quiz and had opted for a string of Bible questions.

On the night I was there with Cyril, he stood in front of the pennies. He mentioned a sum of money and convinced Ednyfed that he had guessed the total value of the coins. Ednyfed praised him. "It's a knack," said Cyril. "I've had banks call on me before now."

"Keep away from that pile, Cyril," said Derwent. "I'll be glad when they come for it." That organiser said, 'Don't touch it, Mr Stamp, I want this bar to yield its last penny's worth of pity before I come to fetch it and count it.' I'm all for charity but the sight of that pile growing like a beanstalk is giving me the creeps." He went into an adjoining bar.

"Derwent is talking a lot of rubbish," said Cyril.

"Why is that?" asked Ednyfed. "How is he talking rubbish?"

I signalled Ednyfed to concentrate on his beer and ignore Cyril who was now stroking the pennies. "Solid as a rock, this pile," Cyril said. "Derwent Stamp may know something about the specific gravity of beer but he doesn't know anything about the gravity of pennies. Did you know that when you place one penny on another you double the weight of both pennies?"

"No," said Ednyfed.

"Fact. And what about the element of magnetism? Do you think Derwent Stamp has taken that into account? And magnetism contributes its own kind of weight, remember that." Ednyfed said he'd remember. "This lot must now weight about a ton. Solid as a rock.

If we had an, earthquake this place would just stay still looking at these pennies. You'd need a demolition squad to dismantle it. Even you, Ednyfed, and you're strong, you could clout that pile with all your might and it wouldn't budge."

Ednyfed was nodding his great head marvelling at these facts. I wanted to denounce Cyril as a loon by exposing the flaws in his physics. But what messages I get from that field of information are muddled. So I left the room instead, advising Ednyfed to get Cyril on to another topic as soon as he could. When I got back, Ednyfed had handed over his mind. Cyril was standing back from the counter with a rapt look and Ednyfed had his hand upraised to deliver the pillar of copper a mighty blow. I shouted at him but his fist had already started out.

The whole room filled with pennies. I ducked. The pile had gone off like a shell. When we recovered from the shock there was no trace of Cyril. I hoped at first that he had been mown down by flying coin, but he had simply done what he always did after creating confusion, gone home. Derwent Stamp kept us there for an hour collecting the pennies and putting them in bags. He even made us count it. I forget the total but it was about twenty pounds less than Cyril's guess.

It was a fortnight before we met Cyril again. He muttered something about the quality of the counter in The Ingle having thrown parts of his theory into shadow.

Ednyfed and I were not vindictive. We were feeling rather cheerful. We had decided, even before that night on all fours, clearing up after Cyril, that our lives needed tidying up. We had each bought a new hat. I had invested heavily. I had bought a magnificent broadbrimmed Austrian article which cost twice as much as I had ever paid for a hat before. Ednyfed's was a slight, dark-brown imitation velour. He loved it. He never seemed to take it off. Some people thought he had joined a local sect that believed in keeping the scalp out of view.

Cyril was anxious to regain Ednyfed's trust. He needed it like food. He stared at Ednyfed's hat. He tried to touch it. Ednyfed shot his head back. When Cyril spoke, it was in his traditional style, in a powerful hiss directed into Ednyfed's ear from a distance of little more than an inch. It put him, ideologically, well inside Ednyfed's skull. I had to lean over drastically to keep the wave-length.

"I know hats," said Cyril. "I had an uncle in Luton and he passed on some vital secrets. I can tell that that's a beauty you've got there, Ed. I can tell by the sheen of the crown and the quality of the stitching. Now that," he pointed at my hat, "is by comparison spurious. Showy, but without the real stuff in it. I could do things to test your hat that I wouldn't dare to do to that one there."

Ednyfed was under the spell again. He made no resistance when Cyril took off his hat. "Now," said Cyril, "this is something I wouldn't care to do to that broad-rimmed article." He gave the hat a powerful tug. The rim came right off. By the time Ednyfed had taken in the full nature of this miracle, Cyril had vanished again.

I don't know who did the damage that set Cyril to limping and wearing his sling. I have no sorrow. I gave Ednyfed my hat. His head is the wrong shape for it. It makes him look overshadowed. But with those brims he might be able to keep Cyril, with his hissing up-to-the-ear style of communication, at more of a distance.

As On A Darkling Plain

In the house of Verdun Pugh, in Khartoum Row, there was a sense of excitement, restrained but still enough to astonish after so long a period of flat calm. During the six weeks that had passed since Verdun had got his first regular job with the local contractor, Hicks the Bricks, he and his Uncle Gomer who also lived with them had been waging a hard war with Grandfather Harris in an effort to persuade the old man that he would be doing himself and them no harm if he vacated the kitchen three or four evenings a week and sat long over a gill at The Plough, the tavern just around the corner from Khartoum Row.

The old man had been obstinate. For years he had sat, so often Verdun had several times to hurry Gomer out of the house lest he use his great strength to lift Mr Harris clean through the fanlight; for years he had sat each evening in that kitchen chair, clad in little more than a collarless flannel shirt and patched trousers, drinking in all the peculiar draughts of evil that life had chosen to send him, draughts, sometimes, of queer, thrilling flavors. He had sat there counting his troubles like beads on a rosary, as black and nearly as tangible. He had also striven to beguile his wretchedness by occasionally detaching his spirit from his body, in accordance with instructions he had once read in a book about Tibet, and sending the thing around the world dropping in on high-class voters and surprising them by lodging formal protests against the condition of sepsis in which his own life and that of his neighbors had entered since the failure of the great strike movements of the Twenties and the onset of mass unemployment.

In that book too he had read of another antic which had added a fine shuddering tassel to the palsy of morbid eccentricities he had worn as a mourning garb since the days of decline had come upon him. It was a specially modulated cry perfected by some sullen votaries in Asia's frozen hills which, repeated often enough on precisely the right key, would open up a distinct hole in the skull of the shrieker. Mr Harris was a tenor of more than fair ability and he had practiced hard to get the exact degree of magic potency that would do the job and let the air in, but he had failed so far. However, he kept trying and one of the few smiles he could still manage was brought by the thought of the look that would be worn by the various agencies that had depressed his life to its present plane of quaint ugliness when he handed them his suffering pate, perforated like a colander, for use as a penholder and a memento of the murderous tomfooleries of waste and inequality to which the substance of Mr Harris had been sacrificially delivered up. He had devoted himself to elaborating a curriculum in misery which would show the world how well it could do along this line when one of its creatures really set out to give it all the help it needed.

To this end, he had eliminated from his life all such light articles as drink, dirty jokes, faith in God, love of women, lounging in the sun on the hillsides, singing in harmony with the boys up by the old grass patch, or anything else that might cause the froth of a forgetful laughter to form upon his heart. This was to be no botched or sloppy job. The coal-owners, the Public Assistance Committee, a whole procession of evictive landlords and a severe hernia having given him an incomparably good start, he was going to go the limit. He would strip his life to one bare board of rigid wretchedness and, that done, he would proceed to ram said board up the rear of the elements who had conspired against his dignity and joy. And maybe one day, when the process would reach its peak, some new creature, like himself in what was good, unlike himself in lacking all weakness and stupidity, would arise from the stirring of a counter-life within the death of his total, organic defeat. To that end, he would sit upon his corner chair until the seat of his pants, or his very own seat itself, gave up the ghost and became unstuck through so much steady sitting.

This program horrified Gomer, especially since Gomer had got his job driving out for the Co-operative store and had taken on an altogether blander view of the social question. Gomer was also courting one of the most vigorous girls in Meadow Prospect, Emma Hall, who was one of the cleaners down at the Coliseum, a picture palace, and who appeared to be kept passionate by having so much to do with warm water, soap and suds. Emma and Gomer were short of a place for their indoor work. Emma had a fleet of older brothers and sisters who used up every inch of floor space with their own activities, and the kitchen in which Mr Harris did his sitting was the only room in Verdun's house which did not have a bare stone floor and Emma had often told Gomer that not even for him would she run the risk of those many complaints that come to those who fool about on the floor with nothing between them and the naked flags. So she threatened him with a jilt unless he could persuade the old man either to clear out or go properly to sleep during their sessions in the kitchen.

Gomer chafed, convinced that Emma, mounting in seed and ungentle at the best of times, would approach the problem from another angle and beat the Yoga to it by treating Mr Harris' skull to a few small holes to be getting on with if he continued to brood over their presence. Gomer told Verdun that no one had the right to be burdening the world with such a long course of meditation and suffering as the old man had sketched out for himself. He had surveyed the old man's seat in the course of several walks around the house immediately in the rear of Mr Harris and he had concluded that it looked a very firm and lasting article, not likely to come unstuck simply by sitting on it. He questioned Verdun as to what methods existed of hurrying this unsticking other than waiting for the element in the case to sit it off.

Verdun admitted to having read of one man who unscrewed his seat by rubbing his hand vigorously around his navel for thirty days and nights in reaction to some long idleness caused by a spasm on the world market, but he doubted if such a ticklish and querulous voter as Mr Harris would consent to sit down and be rubbed for so great a length in so systematic a way. Gomer had also found an item in the paper which told of how some voter in one of the Northern valleys had not just one uncle, like Gomer, living with him, but two. These uncles, being aged and cantankerous, had set about balking and hindering the urges of the young voter in any number of cunning ways such as lying to women about his real nature and even grating some cheap soap into his roasted cheese. These manoeuvres had exhausted the voter who had not minded about the lying because he did a bit in that line himself but he hated cheap soap outright. He had persuaded the uncles to buy an axe. They, though mean, had clubbed together to this end, moved by the cruel notion that the nephew, given an axe, might delight them by chopping a leg off. But the young voter had a subtle plan. This plan was no other than to set about the uncles with the axe and, encouraged by the very good marksmanship he showed from the beginning, he changed the look of the uncles so much they did not now recognize each other.

This was the kind of simple tale that Gomer liked, full of vigour and climax and moral and he read it out five nights running to the old man, letting his voice rise to a bawl that nearly deafened Verdun when he came to the phase of butchery and revenge; and he openly stated when the reading was done, tapping Mr Harris on the knee to make sure that he had his full attention, that if the element in the Northern valley had had four uncles, all of the same bleak quality as the first two, he still would not have had one tithe of the reason that Gomer had for making towards the axe and getting Mr Harris in the sights.

But not even this recital had shifted any part of the expression of scorn that had settled like a snow-cap on the grandfather's face ever since they had started upon him with their request that he vary his life a little.

"To the end. To the end," he said, causing Gomer to turn to Verdun and say that jail was so little worse than this he was wondering whether he would take a swing at Mr Harris there and then with whatever weapon came to hand.

But it was Verdun, addressing a quiet, sincere appeal to the old man and pointing out to him how well the ruling groups were doing already in spreading gloom without any suggestions from Khartoum Row to thicken the mixture that persuaded Mr Harris to break his syllabus of vindicative brooding. He accepted the offer that Verdun and Gomer should club in enough to send him to The Plough three times weekly, twice for a pint, once for a gill. Wednesday was fixed as the opening date of the new era, giving Mr Harris a whole day in which to prepare his spirit for the strangeness of entering a place of public entertainment for the first time in eleven years. Gomer was overjoyed, and angered Mr Harris by standing in front of him and engaging in a lot of gross mimicry of drunken men. This was to show how happy Gomer was at the prospect of Mr Harris taking to drink and a less thoughtful, more chuckling viewpoint, leaving Gomer free to spread out over the whole kitchen with Emma.

"You knock them back, boy," said Gomer. "Don't think of the

expense. Life's short, knock them back and have a good time."

"Oh go to hell," said Mr Harris, half sorry that he had let Verdun talk him out of his ancient austerity. "I pity that Emma, Gomer, Honest to God, I pity her."

"Why?" asked Gomer, not depressed by the old man's judgment.

"Because you're like a bull. You're not like a man, you're like a bull."

"Course I am," said Gomer, smiling and pleased. "Least I will be when you go along to The Plough and stop interrupting me when the tide is running at the full with your mumbles and shrieks and spirit-stuff and groaning with the strain of sitting cross-legged."

"I was talking of the brains of a bull," said Mr Harris, speaking very slowly so that Gomer could take it all in without having to sit down and take it in portions.

"What do I want with brains? I spend all my time with horses and Emma, and I haven't heard any of those parties asking for brains yet."

"You'll get wiser, Gomer. One day Emma may weaken. You can't be strong all the time. If you could there wouldn't be any thinking at all going on on this earth. And when she gets weaker she'll get tired of having so much of you hanging about above her and she'll want something with a bit of spirit attached to it. Where will you be then?"

"With the horses, all the time," said Gomer sincerely,

Verdun hurried home from work on the Wednesday evening in time to counteract any unwillingness his grandfather might still feel about breaking the walls of his old isolation. As soon as the meal was over, Verdun smiled broadly and encouragingly across the table.

"Now, what about changing, Granch?"

"Changing what?"

"Your clothes. You look a bit rough as you are."

"I've looked like this for fifteen years. Get used to it, boy, and stop being fussy."

"But you're going to The Plough tonight. Fresh start, remember? You're going to have a drink and be happy."

"Oh aye, that. I'm sorry I ever said I'd go."

"Don't say that, Granch. You said you'd go. You've still got your best clothes in the upstairs drawer. You'll look a treat. You'll surprise everybody."

"No doubt about that. They're funeral clothes upstairs."

"They look fine. That night you tried them on for me they looked fine."

"All right then," said Mr Harris, averting his eyes shyly from Verdun's. "Let's get them on before that Gomer comes in. He's the most barbaric voter I'll ever meet. I can't bear the noise he makes. If ever he starts to stoop it won't be because of age like it is with me. It'll be because his traffic with the Co-op and Emma will be turning him into a horse full time."

"There's no harm in Gomer, Granch. Wallace the Chips for whom I do odd jobs at night and who is as pensive as you are, says Gomer is the only element he knows who came out of the long slump with more gonads than he went in."

They made their way upstairs. In the bottom drawer of the chest in Mr Harris' room were the suit, bowler hat and starched shirt-front. The suit was black and of a material thicker than any Verdun had seen in use among his own contemporaries. Verdun had never seen very much in the way of elaborate garments and this suit of his grandfather, for all its creeping suffusion of rusty green around his shoulders, struck him as being admirable.

"You'll look a treat in this," he said again and his grandfather grunted.

Verdun put aside the sheet of thin wrinkled white paper that had been covering the clothes. He placed it on the floor with a slow reverence, as if everything connected with this funeral splendour merited its dose of considerate care.

"Ginger it up a bit there, Verdun," said Mr Harris. "You're treating that suit as if it were a mummy." Verdun laid the trousers on the bed. He surveyed the exteme narrowness of the leg.

"Anything missing from these, Granch?"

"How can anything be missing from trousers? Either they are there or not there. These are on the bed."

"They look very thin."

"That was the style when I was younger."

"Were the people thinner?"

"No, just the trousers. We fancied them that style. You had to be very nimble to get into them."

"Think you can manage it now?"

"With a bit of help from you."

"All right then. Here they are."

Mr Harris slipped off his old trousers. They were an old pair of Gomer's and slipped away from the old man's legs as soon as he touched the buttons, as if glad to be on the move. He kicked them away from him and thrust one leg masterfully into the black ones. His foot got stuck half-way down the pipe of cloth and he plunged forward dangerously. Verdun caught him as he was falling, propped him against the bed and told him not to be so daring until he got into the full rhythm of it.

"Have another try, Granch," he said tolerantly. "And it would be a big help if you took off your boots first." Verdun gave him a hand with the boots and after three of four false starts, with Mr Harris falling on him suddenly from different directions, he saw the old man's feet appear through the bottoms.

"They're terrible things to get into, Granch. What was the point of making them so narrow?"

"So that people could really look as thin as they were. That way, such voters as the Relieving Officers who give food grants on behalf of the Council when cannibalism is in sight could see without poking at you that you were as lean as you said you were on the official form."

"Must have given the boys a lot of trouble getting into them."

"A lot. It was nothing to see some voter with big feet stumbling all the way down the street with his trousers only half on and boys from the chapels running behind asking him what the hell he was up to. Sometimes if there was a big funeral and we were all getting dressed up we took turns at holding the trousers still while the rest pushed. Even without the interesting flavour of death, the good harmonies around the grave and the slices of ham at the funeral tea, it was a good way of passing a day on, with not too great a rub of grief across the heart."

"They must have taken a lot of time burying people, with the mourning voters having to go to all this fuss and bother getting their legs covered."

"There wasn't so much speed or crowding in those days. The voters could breathe without having to tell anybody or wonder if it was their turn." He looked down. "I feel queer in these trousers, Verdun."

Verdun stepped back to take a good look. He agreed with the way his grandfather felt. Standing there, with his baggy flannel shirt surmounting the two black columns of mourning cloth, he looked as if he were waiting for a fresher, whiter pair of legs.

"They look fine, Granch. Thin, but fine. Now, what about this contraption?" He held up the starched front. It looked to Verdun like a pair of hand shears. "They look tricky and no mistake. On what part of you do you wear these?"

"Around my neck and over my chest."

"For colds?"

"No. To make me look as if I have a white shirt."

Verdun looked astonished at this. He had never before come into contact with this particular form of fooling the public. In his day it had become enough not actively to show the pelt.

"Let's try the bowler first," said Mr Harris. "We'll leave the front till last. They're terrible things to put on. If they come loose the sharp points can stab you to death. In the funerals in the old days when sorrow among the voters was a lusher article altogether, there were always two first-aid men standing by to heal blokes hurt by fronts that broke loose during the swelling of the hymns. If I can't manage to fix this one on, you can take it along to The Plough and leave me looking stiff in the drawer."

"Oh we'll manage, Granch. I'm looking forward to seeing you in this front. Here's the bowler."

Mr Harris took the hat, a sinister and tall-crowned item. "Top price," he said in a softer voice. "I made a splash on this. I had worked four shifts in a row and this is what I spent most of the money on."

"It's a beauty, Granch. I can see that."

"When I wore this they always put me among the official mourners behind the hearse. That was to give the turn-out a better look. So most times I wore my cheap bowler to be with the rest of the boys. With the mourners I had to look sad all the time and say, 'It was a blessing.' That didn't suit me because I only went for the hymns and sometimes for the ham." He gave the bowler a sharp, sudden rap against the bed rail that made Verdun jump.

"What's that for, Granch?"

"Get the dust out."

"Thought you were trying to get the crown off," said Verdun relieved.

Mr Harris put on the bowler cautiously. It slipped with a kind of audible satisfaction to within a fraction of an inch of his eyebrows. His face became impassively suspicious. He held his head quite still.

Verdun looked at him inquiringly. There seemed to be only a tiny zone of light between the descending shadow of the bowler and the mounting threat of the razor-thin trousers.

"Stop lifting your eyebrows, Granch. They're up too near the bowler."

"I'm not lifting them. It's the bloody hat has swollen. This is one of that Gomer's tricks. He's been wearing it to show off to that Emma and now he's made it too big for me."

"No, honest, Granch. Nobody's touched it."

"Then what the hell is it doing covering my face like a mask? I'll have to bend down to see under the damned thing."

"Perhaps your skull has shrunk."

"Why in the Almighty's name should it do that? A skull doesn't go in and out. It stays."

Mr Harris picked up the tissue paper from the floor, rolled it and fitted it inside the hat. As he was doing so the heavy tread of Gomer was heard downstairs. He was obviously in a state of high tide with regard to noise and merriment. He kept bawling Verdun's name. Verdun went to the bedroom door and shouted down that they were upstairs. Gomer bounded up the stairs promptly and advanced on the grandfather, who had just put the bowler back on, with a look of gleaming wonder in his eye. It was the mourning trousers that had Gomer's attention riveted.

"Oh, you'll surprise them, boy," he started to shout. "You're fit for courting, honest to God. If you didn't look so much like a duck with being so sad and bandy, me and Verdun would have to come with you to drive the women off. Put the coat on now, Uncle Edgar. It's too black for my fancy but, honest to God, it makes me respect you."

"Gomer," said Mr Harris — looking and sounding for all the world like one of his revered Lamas hurled after a lifetime's single-minded concentration on the curved flights of the self-immolating spirit into renewed contact with the rougher forms of man's buffoonery — "Gomer, for Christ's sake, get hold of that counterpane, stuff about a yard of it into that big mouth and chew hard until you come to the dye. Now stand back and give my grandson Verdun a bit of room to help me on with the front."

Gomer, chastened by a fear of offending the old man and postponing the delight of a free and empty kitchen, sat on the bed and stared at Mr Harris' trousers, thinking that the reference to the front had something to do with the buttoning up of that garment.

"It's always the same with those old trousers," he said. "Holes too small and buttons too big. But don't worry. Those boys at The Plough don't care a damn. Very easy going about the fly if you see what I mean."

Mr Harris saw no irrelevance in this, only another clear sample of Gomer's lack of reason.

Verdun advanced on his grandfather from the back, bearing the starched front in his hand. The front was a novelty to Gomer and he bent forward to watch this manoeuvre more closely.

"What the hell are you playing at there, Verdun?" he asked. "You giving the old man a trim or what?"

The collar fitted around the neck.

"It's to look like a white shirt," said Verdun.

"Oh, instead of a waistcoat," said Gomer and winked seriously at the old man as if complimenting him on this resourcefulness.

"Who in God's name would wear this contraption instead of a waistcoat?" asked Mr Harris. "This goes under the waistcoat, you mule."

"I had that at the back of my mind," said Gomer amenably.

"Granch," said Verdun, "how are we going to get these long wings or fins or whatever you call them to stay down?"

"Studs," Verdun. "You're supposed to have studs. A lot of ignorance has come upon this house since life started to smell and I lost the way of laughing."

"Where are they?"

"In the drawer."

"Not there now."

"Do without them."

"How?"

"The waistcoat'll hold them down."

"Aye, aye, of course," said Gomer. "Get the waistcoat, Verdun. Don't see why all you want this fuss with studs." He stood up busily. "Such things are fancy beyond."

Mr Harris drew on his waistcoat. He buttoned it up. It touched his chest at no point. The upper part of his body must have shrunk by a half. Behind the slack the wings of the front jutted sharply, aggressively.

"Fasten the waistcoat up in the back," said Gomer. "There's room for two more blokes in the front here."

Mr Harris and Verdun stood silent. Neither attempted to question or to expostulate with Gomer as to the nature of this new development. Both, the old man and the young, had this habit of doffing their hats respectfully to the Life Force when it seemed to them to be reaching up to a phase of roaring and inexplicable daftness. They regarded Gomer at that moment as the agent of some new revelation in the crass, some new strand in the great rich tapestry of the sardonic and both would have been conscious of a sense of undignified betrayal if they resisted even an attempt by Gomer to solve the question of the protruding wings by stringing the grandfather up on the lintel.

"Undo that waistcoat." Mr Harris did so. Gomer bent forward efficiently and threw the cord's loose end around Mr Harris' torso, drew the cord tightly around the front's bottom half and made a secure knot in the back. Mr Harris stood passive and suffering, his torso inclined slightly forward and expressing reaction to the unaccustomed pressure on his chest by sticking his tongue out as if he were beginning to choke.

"All right, Granch?" asked Verdun, watching the tongue.

"All right. Thank you, Gomer, my boy. I'd never have thought of that, honest. Maybe due to my not having any horses to play about with as you have, but I don't think along simple lines any more. This is fine. You've got me properly trussed, waiting to be plucked. I bequeath my feathers to the broad anus of the last reactionary so he can fly down to hell in comfort. Only one thing you did wrong, Gomer. You should have gone the whole hog and strapped me to the bed post for good so that I and you and Emma would have even less to worry about than we have now."

"Get his coat on, Verdun. That's a pretty big knot I made in the middle of his back and it'll make him feel strange and bitter for a while."

Verdun helped Mr Harris into his coat. He marvelled at the stiff stillness of the old man's frame as this was done. He glanced behind to make sure that Gomer, as Mr Harris had jestingly suggested, had not lashed him to the bed frame.

"A toffee apple," said Gomer, impressed, walking slowly around his fully dressed uncle. "Oh, Jesus, though, this is something to watch. This beats the switchback at Barry. This beats that Royston Richards and his Romanies who play gypsy music down at the Palaceum dressed in yellow shirts. All right, Granch. You're ready.

Walk."

Mr Harris did not move. A twitching around his neck muscles seemed to show that he had the will to walk but he did not budge an inch.

"He's got the cramps," said Gomer."That contraption with wings is cold on his belly, no doubt, and it's given him cramps."

"What have you done to me, Gomer, you stupid sod?" wailed the old man. "I can't move. I seem to be up against a wall. This front and that rope you used are against me like a wall. I'm on to you, Gomer. That talk about The Plough was just camouflage. You've got no intention of letting me out of the bedroom. You've paralyzed me. It's that knot in the back. Get me out of this, you donkey."

"It's all right, Uncle Edgar. It's nerves, that's all. That's what's the matter. You've got out of the way of being dressed-up and blithe after all those years of brooding on the revolution and seeking solace in those antics from India and Tibet. Those habits are enough to give any voter a chill on the guts, even without that front. Take his other arm, Verd."

And between Gomer and Verdun the unresisting grandfather was more or less air-borne down the stairs.

In the kitchen, Verdun's friends, Sylvanus, Merlin and Elwyn were waiting for him. The sight of Mr Harris dressed up in a black suit and a bowler would have caused a stir among the boys at any time but the old man's dramatic entrance between Gomer and Verdun, his feet about three inches off the ground, caused them all to crowd around to take a look at the details. Mr Harris shook himself loose and went to stand in one of the kitchen's further corners, a look of defiance on his face and the same paralytic crouch in the slope of his torso. He was still feeling a captive between the pressure of the shirt front on his chest and Gomer's double knot at the back.

Elwyn, who had been studying an illustrated weekly in the arm-chair, started edging towards the old man. It was the bowler that interested him. He had been thinking of buying one. He knew it would be idle making a formal request to Mr Harris that he be allowed to handle and examine the article. He knew how touchy Mr Harris was about such things. His idea was to get his hand in quickly and examine the hat swiftly in the few seconds taken by Mr Harris to raise his own hand for a retaliatory smack. He shot his arm out and Mr Harris bounded back out of range. He had evidently, for all the concentrated stiffness of his posture, been keeping an eye on Elwyn.

"None of that," he shouted snappishly."No respect for the dead, that's what's wrong with all you silly young sods."

"Who's dead, Mr Harris?"

"Somebody, or I wouldn't be wearing this turn-out."

"Stop badgering him, Elwyn," said Verdun.

"I wanted a quick feel at his bowler. Wanted to test it for weight, honest. I'm thinking of buying one to go with the striped suit my mother's getting for me through the Clothing Club, shilling a week."

"Why is he bent like that?" asked Merlin. "What's he crouching for, Verd?"

Merlin began to walk around the old man who pursed his lips hostilely and kept his hand tight on his hat.

"Don't any of you go touching this bowler," said Mr Harris."It's stuffed with paper to make up for all the wear and tear on my poor bloody skull through the years of stoppage and disaster. One touch and the whole lot comes down like a curtain, blinding me. Leave it alone."

"Come away from there," Merlin, said Verdun, appealingly.

"But why's he crouched like that?"

"It's that white contraption he's got on. It's stiff and fancy and he's not used to it."

"What's it supposed to be?"

"It's a false shirt."

"What's false about it?"

"It's not all there."

"Where's the rest of it?" Merlin looked interestedly at the old man as if he expected him to go producing the rest of this shirt in bits from his pockets.

"It's false," said Verdun."There isn't any more of it."

"Cheap shirt. Cold, though."

"He's got another shirt under it."

"Oh, and it crouches him up?"

"That's it. You're very slow at seeing things tonight, Merlin."

"You can't tell about these things, Verdun."

"What you mean, you can't tell. I saw Granch put the front on. I saw Gomer strapping it down with cord and that's why he's a bit bent. When he gets used to it or Gomer loosens the knot, he'll straighten up and he'll be one of the smartest sights in Khartoum Row."

"I don't know. My old man took to crouching after that big cut in the dole in 1931. And he landed up with what is called a sleeping nerve which makes him wink all the time and look wise as hell. Perhaps your grandfather has got the same kind of trouble coming his way." Merlin bent down and began to study Mr Harris' right eye for any sign of this new disturbance.

"For Christ's sake, stop staring at me, boy," shouted Mr Harris, "or you'll be sleeping. Not just your nerve. All of you."

"Stop aggravating him, Merlin. Come on, Granch. Time to go."

"Where's he going?" asked Sylvanus who was sitting on the table looking at some photographs of a drinking party in Mayfair and feeling rather pleased that Mr Harris, in however rough a fashion, was trying to jerk the standard of dress in Khartoum Row a little nearer the level of the male drinkers in the photographs who had clearly heard little of the Social Insurance which so many of the voters in Khartoum Row used to keep body and soul in a shifting, grimacing truce.

Gomer came in from the backyard with a cane brush and started sweeping hard at the fireside mats. He did the job too vigorously, shifting the main mat a foot every time he made a stroke.

"What's he up to?" asked Elwyn, dodging quickly out of the way to prevent his legs being knocked from under him by the advancing brush-head.

"He's preparing the mat for Emma," said Verdun.

"Is he going to give her the mat?"

"No. She's going to lie on it, so Gomer hopes."

The boys all looked at Gomer with a new wonder. Until then they had thoughts of mats only in relation to the feet. They were grateful to anyone who provided them with a new dimension of utility, even Gomer.

"We're going as far as The Plough, with Granch," said Verdun. He turned and added a word of explanation for his friends. "Granch hasn't been out for a long time. We've been telling him he only lives once and he ought to lead a brighter life. So he's going to The Plough in his funeral suit."

"Good idea, that," said Elwyn. "There are a lot of stern elements in Meadow Prospect who could do with such a new outlook. There's that Octavious Pugh, father of Elvira Pugh, my girl. He's gone jingles with being so pure of mind and he comes at me like a tiger every time I go around courting."

"Coming, Gomer?"called Verdun.

"Course I'm coming. This is the happiest moment I've had for a long time. We'll make a real procession out of it and give Khartoum Row something to remember."He threw his brush down and took hold of his coat. "Something to remember. Won't we, Uncle Edgar?" He slapped Mr Harris hard on the back, at the very spot where he had tied the knot.

"Oh God in Heaven," said Mr Harris in a soft voice on which was falling a thickening shadow of anguish. "Do that again, Gomer, my boy. You didn't quite drive it in. You boys do me a favour, will you? Stand around me as I walk down the street. This is a peculiar thing I'm doing, sort of rising from the dead. It feels hardly decent somehow. Stand around me, hide me a bit until we get to The Plough. If the people see me dressed like this they won't know what the hell is coming off." His voice dropped and it was only Verdun who heard him. "I'm full to the scalp of laughing bloody ghosts. Can you hear them, boy?"

"No, Granch, I can't. It's the creaking of the suit. It's stiff. Get around him, boys. You get in front, Gomer."

The little bank set forth down the gully, Mr Harris in the middle shrinking down to a point where only the top of his bowler was visible. Gomer in front was grinning to the widest possible degree and bearing himself with a bursting pride similar to that of a homecoming animal-catcher bringing something back alive. Verdun observed that a strand of the white tissue paper inside his grandfather's bowler was beginning to slip out at the back. In the half-light of the evening it had a curious effect, giving Mr Harris' appearance at the top a quaint compromise between saint and Foreign Legionnaire.

Through the veins of Mr Harris, made narrow and cold by a too long acceptance and inertia, crept the intimations of a renascence which could have no meaning, for which he could feel no love, plucking stealthily and with tremendous pain. They reached The Plough, a squat, detached building at the end of the street, large but invested now with a quiet frowsiness. The contingent stopped outside the main door. They had all fallen silent during the last half of the walk, conscious that what they were doing had something of a ceremonial character. They all looked and felt deeply solemn, like the inhabitants of an extremely Northern bay seeing a boat steam into their harborage after months of half-starving sequestration. The symbolism of the moment was vivid to every mind present. An expression of climactic and passionately reminiscent melancholy was contracting the features of the old man. Even the animal grossness of Gomer became sensitive for a few strange quivering instants. He walked up to Mr Harris and shook him by the hand. The boys did the same and then turned away. Quickly and silently the old man was left alone.

Thy Need

Whit-Monday was the first day of brilliant sun after a week of mist and rain. Spring was nearly always a wet, diffident affair in the hills around Meadow Prospect and the people were delighted to see the burst of sun, for this Monday was a day of festival and gala. The sixth annual sports day organized by the Constitutional Club was being held. The club flag was at the top of its pole, washed and fresh. The junior section of the club had its wooden premises decorated and filled with tables for the tea that was to come off at five that afternoon, and from about noon there had been groups of members' children hanging about the club's front door getting their teeth ready for the start. With these young elements circling for the swoop, Meadow Prospect wore an even hungrier, more watchful look than usual.

Most of the day's sporting events were over when the three friends, Sylvanus, Verdun, and Elwyn sat down on a bench in Meadow Prospect square, near the spot where Lodovico Facelli had his ice-cream barrow. It was getting warmer all the time. The boys had their best suits on and were wearing the tight, white, long-peaked collars which were the current fancy among the young of the district. Their faces were red under the strain of strong sun and slow strangulation. Verdun ordered three threepenny wafers from Lodovico. The Italian made them extra-thick and, after having handed them over, leaned on the barrow and stared at the boys as if the sight of them gave him genuine pleasure. Lodovico was considered too dreamy and generous to have much of a future in business, but he seemed to manage. Verdun waved his hand genially at Lodovico every now and then to show that the kindness of his expression and the thickness of his wafers were not wasted.

"What you boys been racing in?" asked Lodovico.

"We've been stewards."

"Stewards? What you do?"

"We were doing little jobs for Mr Marsden, who is the brains of the Con Club. If Mr Marsden sees anything that needs knocking into the ground, like a nail or a stake or some voter who won't listen to the judges, he gives us the mallet and the signal to proceed."

"So you wait for the tea now?"

"There's one more race, the last of the day. The walking race, said Sylvanus. My uncle Onllwyn is entered and he's going to blind them with science."

"He good?"

"They used to call him the White Horse, on account of his long snowy drawers and his fine strong stride, said Verdun. He's got a trick in starting, too, a way of twisting his legs and shooting forward like a bullet that is magic. It'll make it useless for the other blokes even to get off the mark. The start is important, because this race is short. Honest, Lodovico, I feel sorry for those other boys when I think of Uncle Onllwyn and the way he shoots off. I've seen him practising in the back lane when things are quiet and I know. I call him the White Flash, because all you see is dust and his butts getting smaller. It'll be a big day for him, too, because things have never gone right for Uncle Onllwyn, and this is the first walking match they've held here, and he's never had the chance to shine before."

"I hope he win," said Lodovico. "I know Onllwyn. He's a kind old voter. He's sympathetic."

"He'll win all right," said Verdun. "Tell Lodovico about the dung, Syl."

"Oh, no," said Sylvanus. "That's supposed to be a secret, and anyway Lodovico wouldn't want to hear about a thing like that, not with him in such a clean line of trade as ice-cream."

"Dung?" said Lodovico, still smiling intensely at the boys, but clearly puzzled. "Is this why they call your uncle the White Horse?"

"No. I'll tell you. Onllwyn heard about a famous runner called Gito who once lived among these hills. He was fleet as a bird, that Gito. Started after sheep and caught hares, that sort of voter. Uncle Onllwyn, who is a great reader, came across an old book about Gito, and it said Gito kept so supple by sleeping on a bed of old dung. So Onllwyn made a long coffin-shaped box and half-filled it with dung, and that's where he's been sleeping for the last week, in this box in the shed behind the house, getting suppler all the time. He was so supple after the second day he was waving about like that flag over the Con Club."

"Good God," said Lodovico. "He must be very poor. Not even in Italy they sleep in dung. But I hope he win."

"That is certain, Lodovico, because in addition to being supple he also has his grips, home-made countraptions of solid rubber that he fits into his mouth to bite on whenever he feels his wind coming a bit short."

"Don't tell him about those," said Sylvanus. "He's in a fog now after what you told him about Onllwyn sleeping in the box."

"Those grips are more interesting than the dung, I reckon. He looks full of grip when he's got them fitted in and his teeth seem to come right out at you. Between you and me, I think they called uncle Onllwyn the White Horse as much for his look as for his stride or his drawers."

"What Onllwyn going to do with the money he win?" asked Lodovico.

"He's got that all worked out. He's buying gardening tools. He's been very keen to get some of those for a long time. He spends so much time staring into the window of Phineas Morgan the Iron-monger that Morgan has got into the way of giving Onllwyn one flick with the dusting rag for every two he gives the window. Onllwyn wants these tools because he is keen on the earth and wants a smallholding. So long, Lodovico. We're off to the 'Little Ark', that pub down at the bottom of Gorsedd Row."

"You drink?"

"No. The race starts from there. It's the landlord of the 'Little Ark', Hargreaves, who's giving the prize. It'll be the first time Onllwyn ever made anything out of the drink trade."

The three friends made their way towards the 'Little Ark'. It was one of the older taverns of Meadow Prospect, low-roofed, a rust-red in colour. From a distance they could see Hargreaves the landlord standing in the small cobbled yard which fronted it, giving greeting to the first entrants and their supporters. The boys saw Onllwyn coming towards them down a side street. Verdun and Sylvanus looked at him wonderingly, for the last time they had seen him he had been radiant and lithe, with a hint of mastery in his every word and step. Now he walked slowly and his face was thoughtful and shadowed even beyond the point of darkling pensiveness normal in Meadow Prospect. In his right hand he carried the cheap suitcase which contained his racing equipment. They waited for him to come up with them.

"What's up, Uncle Onllwyn? What are you looking so sad for? You bad?"

"No. I'm all right. I feel quite painless."

"You look down in the dumps. Come on, Uncle Onllwyn. I've been telling everyone what a champion walker you are. We've been telling everybody that you're going to win."

"I'm not going to win. There are many things that are certain. One is, I'm not going to win."

"The bookies have been at him," said Elwyn, who knew more about these things than his friends.

"You and your bookies," said Onllwyn, looking at Elwyn with a calm contempt. "It'll all be due to Cynlais Moore, if you want to know."

"Cynlais, the bloke with the limp?"

"He's got a bit of a limp. That's the boy. He came to see me two days ago. Cynlais seemed to be in the deepest sorrow I have ever seen. You know how I get when I see somebody in sorrow."

"You go daft, Uncle Onllwyn." Sylvanus's tone was sharply unpleasant. "You'd be better off deaf when the sorrowful come around. But why ever did you listen to Cynlais Moore? Cynlais is known to be the biggest liar in Meadow Prospect."

"Cynlais is alive. Men alive change. It is likely that truth may have come to a better understanding with Cynlais."

"All right then. If you don't want to get on, that's your look-out. There's too much to pity in you. You're a clown for stroking the sorrowful, that's your trouble."

"He came to me and told me about his wife, Elvira Moore, who has been ill for a long time and is taking up a lot of money in tonics. Her bill from the chemist makes the Social Insurance look very trivial, says Cynlais. So he wants to make some money. He also has a young son called Maldwyn Moore. This boy has a fine soprano voice and drives people half mad with religious fervour and the wish to be off on a crusade with his rendering of such songs as 'Jerusalem, Jerusalem'".

"I've heard that Maldwyn," said Verdun. He had never heard Maldwyn sing a note. He wished only to counter Onllwyn's current of thoughtless compassion. "He's ronk. He sings like a frog. Cynlais was on form with you, Uncle Onllwyn. Mostly he tells the truth about just one item on the list to keep his hand in, but with you he seems to have gone the whole hog."

"Boys change. He may now be like a lark, this Maldwyn. So an uncle who lives in London tells Cynlais that there are fine openings for young Welsh boy sopranos in those parts. The voters are making big money in that quarter, and they like listening to these boys sing when they are getting tender over their drink. But this Maldwyn is ragged. He likes going down slopes on his backside, and he takes the seat out of a pair of trousers as quickly as you would say hullo. So if Cynlais gets enough money he is going to pack Maldwyn off to London, where he can make a fortune singing, and where it's flat, so that he won't forever have to be putting money in patches. So Cynlais argued me into letting him win this race."

"Of all the nerve! Honest, Uncle Onllwyn, you're being silly. Are you forgetting the way you were crying and trembling with excitement when you first read about this Gito the fleet one, and how you said he was the boy who ought to have been the patron saint of the Celts because he was one voter who would have shown nothing but speed and scorn to the Saxons and the coalowners when they came around for their collection of scalps and profits. And are you forgetting the trouble you had waiting for bits to fall off every coalhouse in the street so that you could build the box which let you try out Gito's recipe of the dung?"

"He's been bewitched by this Moore, if you ask me," said Verdun. "They say this Moore is such a liar he hasn't even given the same reason for his limp twice."

"He knows I'm the best walker about here. He's heard from somebody who used to live down in Carmarthen about how I would go flashing about down there beating all the other boys with my skill and stamina. And he said, 'If anybody's got the knowledge and the craftiness to win me the prize, it's Onllwyn Evans.'"

"But didn't you tell him you needed gardening tools just as much as Elvira needs tonics or Maldwyn needs trousers to sing to the voters in London?"

"Mine is a selfish wish. I want tools, a smallholding, and the feel of fertile earth for myself. But Cynlais wants the things he wants for others. He made me feel a bit ashamed."

"So what did you say you'd do for this crook?"

"I told him I would show him all the secrets of victory. I spent two hours the night before last teaching him the special leg-twisting starting method which made such a mock of all those elements in the western counties who were tempted to take the road against me. Cynlais got himself into a five-ply knot to start with, he being such an amateur and having that smack on the leg, besides being very eager for a triumph. But after I had unwound him about six times and given him a lot of encouragement he got into the way of it, and now you can't even stop to talk to the man without having him suddenly bend down and shoot off like a torpedo to show his mastery. For all his limp that Cynlais can move in a handy way."

"Of course he can. That Cynlais is a bigger crook than any of those boys we see in those serials down at 'The Dog' scheming and burgling weekly and paying no rent. That limp is only something he puts on to fool people and flood tender-hearted elements like you with tears. I bet he hasn't even got a wife called Elvira or a kid called Maldwyn."

"Oh yes, he has. I've seen them, and they're in the exact condition described by Cynlais: Elvira pale as a ghost and scooping up Oxo direct from the pot every whipstitch, and Maldwyn very vocal in a high-pitched way and as bare-breeched for lack of cloth as a cat."

"What else did you teach him? Don't tell me you let him into that ancient secret of Gito's, of how to be supple though old and bent nearly double most of the time. You know what a great comfort having that secret has been to you through the years."

"At first I wasn't going to tell him. But honest, Sylvanus, he looked so pathetic, and his legs and arms creaked so much when he moved I had to shout my directions at him. So I thought that if Gito lived only to silence the joints of this Cynlais he did not live in vain, so last night I granted him the use of the box and he slept in it.

"Well, I hope that's the last thing you'll do for him. You'll never get on, Uncle Onllwyn. You've got no guile, no hardness at all. You chuck away your trumps, and to the last day of time you'll be nothing but a mat for the voters, being taken in by elements like Cynlais Moore."

"I'm letting him have the grips as well."

"Oh no! The mouth grips? Why, they are the best thing you've got."

"He'll have to have them if he's going to win. If there's one thing that makes a man sure of victory it's those grips. They make a man feel he's got the world itself in the palm of his hand and wondering where to throw it. It would have been heartless showing Cynlais the leg-twist, the secret of the dung, and then keep back the grips which are the very crown of all my paraphernalia."

They heard Hargreaves shouting on the entrants to come in and get dressed for the start. Hargreaves was the starter and was swinging a pistol in his hand. He looked full of drink and malice, and the friends approached him from behind. There were some very old men among the entrants, for the minimum age was forty. Some of them had already changed, and the ancient, withered look of their limbs and their obvious unfitness to stand up to anything much more than the sound of Hargreaves' gun made Verdun and Sylvanus all the more bitter about the gesture of self-denial that Uncle Onllwyn had been talked into by Cynlais Moore. Several of the men were being served with beer by Mrs. Hargreaves in the narrow passageway of the 'Little Ark'.

"Where's Cynlais?" asked Verdun.

"Oh, he'll be here shortly. You'll be able to tell him by the easy springy way of walking he'll have. After a night in the dung-box, Gito's casket, you feel so springy you think all the time you're on the point of floating, and when gladness comes into the heart to supplement the suppleness of your limbs, you have to press hard on your feet to keep on the earth at all. That Gito must have been the son of the wizard Merlin."

A man in his middle forties with very red thick hair and a face which in normal mood would have been smooth and cheerful came around the corner. But his face at that moment was neither cheerful nor smooth. There was an expression of settled wretchedness upon it, and he walked slowly, as if every motion of his body was undertaken only after an uneasy chat with pain.

"Either this is Cynlais's dying twin," said Onllwyn, "or he didn't follow the directions as set forth by Gito and me."

"He looks rough," said Sylvanus delightedly. "Looks to me as if you're going to have those gardening tools whether you want them or not, Uncle Onllwyn. It doesn't seem that Cynlais could beat a hearse in his present shape. He looks as if he's been sleeping under and not in the box."

"He'll be a new man when he gets the grips in," said Onllwyn obstinately.

Cynlais had seated himself on a low stone tile that had been let into the garden wall of the 'Little Ark'. When he saw Onllwyn he raised his right arm stiffly and was obviously on the point of some bad-tempered accusation, but he thought better of it, and did no more than sigh in a loud, hopeless way. Cynlais's face had no cunning and these changes of mental front were conveyed in the shift of his eyes and mouth. "You know, Onllwyn," he said quietly, "that my wife Elvira has many troubles. Among those troubles is nerves."

"I know that, Cynlais. I've seen Elvira shake when Maldwyn has come singing at her from behind. It was I who got you that extra large box of the herb skullcap from that nature-healer, Mathew Caney the Cure, to see if it would steady her trembles. But what have Elvira's nerves got to do with the feeble and limping way in which you are walking?"

"It was that box, the casket of Gito, or whatever you call it," said Cynlais bitterly, again making a clear effort to keep his bad temper in the basement of his mood. "You told me to lie in it, so that its healing properties could go healing and refreshing into every joint. When you first told me that, I thought that you were out of your head, made jingles by your years in the solitude dreaming of land and sheep of your own. But I took your word for it even though my first inclination was to turn you over to Naboth Jenks the Pinks and those other boys in the Allotment Holders' Union for wasting a boxful of the prime stuff. But you have a wise, pitying look and I listened. I didn't like the coffin shape you had managed to work on to that box either, but I carried it home, and until Elivra and the kids had gone to bed I kept it in a shed behind the house. When everything was quiet I carried it down to the kitchen, thinking to myself all the time what a sinister shape this box has, and wondering why you hadn't picked a homelier and less haunting pattern. Between the dung and thoughts of doom I was not happy as I laid that article down in front of the kitchen fire, for it was there I put it, determined to be cosy, if foul. Now, as I said, Elvira has nerves, the longest in all Meadow Prospect. These nerves make her twitch and they also make her dream, and she often thinks her dreams show up the future, and it's no joke when listening to Elvira after a night when her dreams have been full of wise bright eyes to see her next week winking away at last week as they thrust freezing fingers up today. It seems a couple of days ago she had a whole belt of dreams about me being kicked by a horse and killed. She had seen me there in her dreams, dead, and apart from me leaving her unprovided for, having been kicked by a horse even poorer than I was and in no way able to make payment for the use of me, she said I had looked quite nice and she had enjoyed the spectacle of me lying there in dreams, stiff as a board and pale as winter. About an hour after I had settled myself in the box, wriggling about and feeling uncomfortable and cursing you and that silly old fool Gito, I doze off. Then Elvira upstairs notices I am not at her side. This worries her, for with all my other failings I am a whale of a man for sleeping in my own bed, so that the boys from the Government will know exactly where to come when they wish to tell me that my days of doubt and trouble are at an end. So I am never far from Elvira's side at night. She catches a slight smell in the air, which, while a common enough smell, is not often to be smelled in our house. The smell of horse. This makes her twitch, with all her nerves working up to a real loud climax of hallelujahs like the boys in the chapels, because she remembers the dream with me catching it from a hoof and being laid flat. She lights a candle, terrified. She comes cautiouusly down the stairs. She opens the kitchen door. Now, I ask you, Onllwyn Evans, if you were less keen on getting back to the land and were in the way of seeing the dead lying about in your dreams, what would you do if you saw what Elvira saw then, me stretched out in what looks like a coffin but which is worse than a coffin because I am resting on a layer of pure waste?"

"I'd blow out the candle for a start," said Uncle Onllwyn, trying to see the problem as best he could from the viewpoint of Cynlais Moore, and sounding very helpful. "I'd do that so that I would see as little of you as possible."

"All right for you to be so wise. Elvira nearly went off her head. She goes off into the loudest laughing fit heard in meadow Prospect, even counting the beaut we had from that burning fanatic Ogley Floyd the Flame when he saw the whole truth about mankind five seconds after having a truncheon broken in three over his pate in the Minimum Wage troubles of 1910. I am standing up in the box now bawling at Elvira that I am simply becoming supple, to read no more into it than that, and telling her to shut up her screeching for God's sake, or she will be bringing down on us a visit from Parry the Pittance, the official who calls on behalf of the County Council to take away the demented. At that moment in rushes Teifion Farr, from two doors down, an interfering toad, a busybody, a man who has tufts of coconut matting lodged in his ear from keeping it so often to the ground listening to the approaching hoof-beat of ca-lamity. Teifion sees the scene in the kitchen and he thinks this is what he has been waiting to see all these years. He thinks I am up to some devilry with Elvira, because he doesn't often see voters standing up naked in the kitchen without even a soap-sud to take the strain, and Teifion is a Calvinist with a low, malicious view of man. He takes hold of me and beats me around that kitchen in a way I hope I will never know again. If I had been a drum he would certainly have got the message across to Calvin. The sound of me being made into pulp brought Elvira to her senses, and for a whole minute she stood there admiring the quick, nimble strokes of Farr as he half-butchered me. Then she remembers about the box as she sees me and Farr running around it for the tenth time. She calls the kids, drags it outside and they burn it, and the back fills up with voters who think from the glow we are celebrating some brand of jubilee or armistice. So that's the end of your box."

"Poor old Gito!"

"Why sympathize with that old goat? He's dead and as used to slowness as the rest of us. Fix your mind on the problems of the quick and the still-vexed, Onllwyn."

"It was better for Gito than for me."

"Why?"

"He didn't have to deal with bunglers and menaces like you."

"Who are you calling a menace? It was your damned coffin that started it all. And I'm still aching from Teifion Farr's treatment. That's why I feel like one half raised from the dead. I reckon you ought to feel keener than ever to let me have this prize, although I don't know how I'm going to beat anybody now with this present feeling upon me. How would you like to win and hand me the money, Onllwyn?"

"No, that wouldn't be honest. I like to see the people do the thing for which they get the pay or the reward. I'm not an all-out Marxist, but I'll go as far as that with those boys in the discussion group at the Library and Institute."

"Don't forget Elvira'll be worse after the shock she got from that box. And when Maldwyn catches the ears of those voters in London he'll pay you the money back five times over."

"Oh, leave him alone," said Verdun to Onllwyn. "This Cynlais is making a fool out of you."

"Now you file off, Harris," said Onllwyn. "Look at all those blokes who've entered. Life has snarled at them all, judging by their look, and they'll have to be carrying each other if they want to advance after the first minute. And you forget that you'll be using my grips. Once you get your teeth in those, boy, you'll forget all about your bruises and failures. They'll give you the fierceness and will to win we elements seem most to lack. They make you feel supple and fleet as if you had made a proper use of Gito's box."

"I bet he put it on the fire himself to save coal," said Elwyn, his eyes settled unblinking and hostile on Cynlais.

"Of course he did," said Verdun. "And I bet that Teifion Farr was never heard of on this earth until a few minutes ago. Whenever Cynlais Moore talks, truth orders a truss."

"Now you three wise young rodneys, file off," said Cynlais.

Cynlais and Onllwyn went off into the back room of the 'Ark'. Onllywn was out again in two minutes wearing his singlet and his curiously long white drawers which caught the eye of his three young friends who had been brought up to think of these articles as either very short or not there at all. He wore a look of solemn responsibility which, taken together with the length of his drawers, made Elwyn laugh out loud. Verdun dug his arm into Elwyn's side.

"Sorry, boy," said Elwyn. "You look fine, Uncle Onllwyn; a treat, honest."

An old competitor, with knicks as long as Onllwyn's, but with limbs much less fitted for racing, came out of the 'Ark's' passage-way, led by a friend. They were both staggering a little, but the man in the drawers was crying as well. They sat down on the stone bench near the door. The boys noticed that the weeping man had a long plain scar running across his brow.

"That's Enoch Vizard," said Onllwyn. "The man with the scar is Enoch. And his friend is Luther Mitchell. I didn't know that Enoch was interested in such events as races. Hullo, Luther, What's wrong with Enoch? He seems to be in trouble."

"He'd be all right if he wasn't so stubborn, said Luther. He makes up his mind to be in this race and there we are. A mule. Just being a mule is bad enough, but a mule within two breaths of the pension is a pitiful sight to see. You know what a fine strong chap Enoch was before he got that smack on his forehead?"

"I remember," said Onllwyn. "He was the pride of Meadow Prospect with his great strength. One never knew what he was going to lift next. He was one of the few men who kept things moving during the great slump."

We got here soon for the changing, and when Enoch took off his trousers to get into his running drawers he became very sad at the thin look of his legs. He said he had seen them before, of course, going to bed and so on, but he had never noticed before how much they had dwindled. The back room of the 'Ark' is a lighter place than any bedroom in Meadow Prospect and full of truth. So I said what the hell, of course we shrink. I even hummed him that well-known hymn which deals with shrinkage and decline in a very clear way. I added that after that bump he got on the boko when the roof came down he ought to be glad he's not bloody well dead. And I said let's have a drink, boy, and to hell with all such antics and dwindling and age and taking off your trousers when the light is too good. So we started to drink. And there we are. When Hargreaves fires off that great gun we'll have to give Enoch a strong shove in the right direction or he'll be landing up in the wrong town, honest to God."

The boys closed around watching Enoch Vizard pulling at the legs of his drawers and sobbing hard as he stroked the thin blotched emaciated skin of his arms and legs.

Cynlais came out. He was wearing tight white drawers that had an elegant cut alongside such baggy articles as those worn by Vizard and Onllwyn, but his vest was a crimson, shapeless effect that looked as if it had been cut down from a dress with the wearer still wearing it and fighting to keep it intact. He appeared self-conscious and furtive, and gave Onllwyn a sly dig as if to say he was now ready for final instructions. Onllwyn paid no attention to him at all. He was staring at Enoch Vizard.

"It would be a good thing," said Onllwyn, "if I could arrange a little victory for Enoch. That poor bloke is half-eaten away by despair. I've had a slow and grinding trip through the mill, it's true, but I haven't yet had my head under a ton of rock like this voter, nor does my skin look as if it has just been knitted on by a poor hand with the needles. It would set him up no end if he could turn out to be the best walker in Meadow Prospect."

"No chance," said Luther Mitchell. "No chance. Very nice of you to offer, Onllwyn. But as soon as Enoch walks a bit too fast that crack across his brow gives him a terrible headache and giddiness, and when he is in that state, I've seen falling stars that were nearer to the earth and easier to manage."

"Very nice of you to offer," said Cynlais ironically, pushing his head fiercely between Luther and Onllwyn. "It's a pity everybody couldn't win. Then you'd be very happy, Onllwyn. A proper mixture of Carnegie and Claus, that's what you are out to become, boy. Come on, for God's sake, and show me the magic of those grips."

Cynlais, Onllwyn, and the three boys moved off conspiratorially around the corner of the 'Little Ark'. Onllwyn brought the grips, large rough-hewn objects, out of his case. Cynlais looked at them astonished. "Where in God's name am I supposed to wear those?"

"Don't be backward, Cyn. In the mouth."

"What kind of a jack will I need to get my head around those? Is this some kind of sombre buffoonery, Onllwyn?"

"No, no. With these in, you'll be breathing deep and easy when all the rest will be gasping their guts out and dreaming of the iron lung."

"But just look at the size of them. Just one half of one of those would fill me. Thinking through the years of that Gito has driven you off the hinge, boy. And I didn't tell you this before, but I've got a very small mouth for a grown man. All the Moores have dainty lips."

"It's the size of the grips that gives them their special quality. That's why I designed them big. You are so busy keeping your mouth around them you pay no heed to the call of fatigue. Once during my fourth year on the Social Insurance, they kept my teeth so occupied I even managed to turn a blind eye to the strong need for death."

"You wouldn't be able to hear any kind of call with those things blocking you up...Wait a minute though..." Cynlais stepped very close to Onllwyn. His eyes narrowed and his nostrils swelled. He was clearly on some crest of cunning insight. Onllwyn blushed and trembled a little in his long drawers.

With so little on he did not like anyone to look quite as infra-red as Cynlais.

"Now I'm up to you," said Cynlais in a rising voice. "I can see through all your tricks now, boy. I didn't think you were so smart, Onllwyn, but lucky for me at the last moment I can see you for the crook you are."

"You're off your head, Cynlais. Buck up, boy. Your thoughts are farther round the bend than normal."

"You're as deep as a snake. Now I see the way you planned it. First of all you see I'm the only one who's got a chance of walking you off your feet. You saw my rightful quality as a walker better than I did myself. You decided early on that I must be driven from the race by hook or by crook. With Cynlais Moore a cripple, you said, Onllwyn Evans need have no fears. When I came to you begging your help you must have thanked God for delivering your victim into your hands instead of having to wait and do the job by breaking my toes quietly whenever you stood next to me in the queue at the Exchange."

Cynlais, his eyes bright, paused here to go back over the details of his first interview with Onllwyn, which were now apparently becoming significant to him for the first time. Onllwyn and the boys, fascinated by the sweep of Cynlais's narrative, sat down to enjoy it the more.

"First," said Cynlais, "there was that amazing caper of the starting method. That should have put me on my guard, but I was blind with worry and want. You got me into as many wriggles as a lizard, then you tell me to shoot myself into straightness. What was that but an outright invitation to all the ruptures among these hills to camp out with Cynlais Moore. Abolish rent, ye ruptures. In Cynlais there are many mansions, and if you find them a bit cramped just give Onllwyn the wink; he's the boy to have Moore walking lower than a duck at all points. But that didn't work. So you rig up that coffin and treat me to a lot of chatter about that element Gito, whom you paint as a model Celt because he could run so fast he would have been able to catch even joy and a steady job in Meadow Prospect. I can see now how you meant the box to work. First, the sight of me in it was to craze Elvira, then with her crazed you would nip in and clamp the lid on, leaving me boxed for evermore and Elvira given the blame, you sly, seeing old sausage. Or I was to suffer some mental breakage from finding myself lower, flatter, and on an odder mattress than I have ever known since the Navy took to oil in the boilers and I took to tinned milk on the table. But that failed too. You didn't count on that best of neighbours and ambulance men, Teifion Farr, who is on permanent duty waiting to find the whole of Khartoum Row pinned beneath the very rump of doom and squealing for splints, tourniquets, and testaments. Now, you come to your third attempt, and it's the cool friendly way in which you hand these various courses to me that makes me marvel. Two bits of rubber big enough to choke a grown bloody elephant, and you ask me to fit them into my mouth. Cynlais was now shaking with anger and disappointment.

"Come on," said Sylvanus to his uncle. "Give your advice and grips to Enoch Vizard, who'll know better than to call you a snake and a crook."

"Wait a minute," said Onllwyn. "Don't be too hard on Cynlais. He's worried about Elvira and self-conscious about turning up here with such tight revealing drawers and a singlet that looks as if it was bitten out of his grandmother's coms. Now calm down, Cynlais and tell me, do you or do you not want to win this race?"

"Course I want to win it. Don't pay any attention to what I said. I was nervous marching about here half-naked and all keyed up. I talked to you like an old rodney. You tell me what to do, Onllwyn."

Around the corner they could hear Hargreaves marshalling the competitors. Onllwyn showed Cynlais the grips once more and once more Cynlais fell back, his face carved into the familiar zones of distrust and horror.

"For God's sake, Onnll., isn't there a way of doing without those?"

"I can't guarantee success without the grips. I've given speed, endurance, and that fleet elusive Gito most of my thought, so don't quibble."

"All right then, block me up." Cynlais turned his back to the boys while Onllwyn helped him to adjust the rubbers.

"This one in the front and the other one a bit more to the back. You get fanatical once you get your teeth deep into these."

The boys waited with great interest to see the result of all the manoeuvres of Onllwyn and the agonized twitching of Cynlais. Only Verdun among the boys had seen Onllwyn with the grips in position, and he was better prepared than Sylvanus and Elwyn to stand the ghastly contortion of Cynlais's face when he turned round. But even he was shocked to see anyone look so much like a cross between a devil-fish and a hell-hound as Cynlais, his mouth painfully yawning and his eyes bursting with the strain of his gaping jaws and ripening indignation. He was letting fly at Onllwyn with a long speech of furious blame, but Cynlais might just as well have been praising Onllwyn up to the skies for all his listeners understood. They led him to the starting-point. Hargreaves, still waving his pistol, looked closely at Cynlais.

"Is this man fit to start?" he asked Onllwyn.

"Fitter than you."

"He's looking as if he's just taken his seat on a spike."

"As long as the spike's not showing there's nothing in the rules against that."

Cynlais took his place between Onllwyn and Enoch Vizard. Enoch was recovering slowly from his drink and grief and was wiping his eyes groaning a little now and then to keep in touch with his receding mood. The first thing he saw when he took his arm down and looked around was the face of Cynlais, spread out in a fashion never before seen in Meadow Prospect, and going dark now with the savage effort of his endurance. Enoch darted from the line and made for the sheltering doorway of the 'Ark'. He was dragged back by Luther Mitchell, who told him that Cynlais was no more than a trick of the shifting light, and also that if Cynlais with his look of being three-quarter strangled was the average sample of athlete entered for this race, then Enoch could afford to dawdle for a round of sobbing at every corner and still win.

Hargreaves was inspecting his pistol. Cynlais was bending down, painfully full of deep, suffering sounds. Onllwyn was busy instructing him in the leg-twists necessary for the bullet-like start. Cynlais was whimpering like a dog now and getting into the most dangerous knot. He was listening too closely to his own welling noises to make any sense of what Onllwyn was telling him to do in the matter of his feet. In his tight drawers his backside was wearing the same expression of staring, mortal, atrabilious strain as his face, and Verdun kept passing from the front to the back of him to get the full flavour of this miracle in two shades. Hargreaves's pistol went off with a great bang, scaring to death what little was left of Cynlais's overwrought wits. With a tremendous shudder his body flattened out on the floor and he passed gratefully into a dead faint, his very last act before the eclipse being a brief look of loathing thrown at Onllwyn. His outflung arm tripped the feet of another competitor, an earnest man in his middle forties, Samuel Howells, and Howells went crashing to the floor and stayed there, unhurt, but with as little wish to move as Cynlais. A lot of these competitors, said Elwyn to Verdun, as they watched this scene, had been pushed into these events by their families who were greedy for money to make an extra trip to such places as that cinema, 'The Dog', and the alert, fit look of this Howells as he lay on the floor making no move to be up and doing proved it.

The others set forth. It was clear from the start that there were only two men in it. Onllwyn and Enoch Vizard. There seemed to be the dynamic of some desperate rage in Enoch, as if he knew that if this were to be the last fling then at least he would be really far-flung at the end of it. Onllwyn had all his work cut out to keep an even yard behind him. Their shoulders were working with a broad ugly swing that struck the eyes of Verdun, who was half running along the pavement, as downright sinister and saddening. They all urged Onllwyn to put a spurt on, warning him that Hargreaves seemed to have slipped a drop of elixir into whatever Enoch had been drinking in the 'Ark'.

"I'll let him win," said Onllwyn. "I wouldn't have the heart to beat him, honest I wouldn't. This will be some sort of crown for his shrinking head." And as he said that he shouted to the unheeding Enoch to slow down a bit and take it easy, to watch out for that weakness in his head, that he was among friends, that after this day's racing the White Flash, with an inch or two on his drawers and a bit less gasp in his average breath, would not be Onllwyn but Enoch Vizard.

Eight minutes after the start twilight cracked down on Enoch. He went deathly pale, raised his hand to his head, and began reeling. Onllwyn and the boys broke into cries of sympathy and encouragement: "Steady up there, Enoch! No need to strain so much at the leash, Vizard."

Even people sitting on their doorsteps who had been watching them without interest, thinking that the sight of voters half-clad and walking at abnormal rates was only another twitch of the long Crisis, now stood up and started to take an interest in the problem of Vizard's zeal and agony. Enoch was staggering on the largest possible scale. Onllwyn did his best to keep him standing, moving forward, and in the race. It was not easy, for Enoch's movements were as tangential and odd as those of a Rugby ball. Onllwyn kept close behind him, supporting him when Enoch showed a tendency to lurch headlong, and dragging him back whenever he went off the official route. Enoch in his bewilderment was going right into houses through doors that were never closed, either because the lines of doors and jamb were no longer parallel, or because the sight of a shut, staring door cooled the sense of community in a place where environment was already causing the blood stream of most voters to slow down and stop taking the thing so seriously. On two occasions Onllwyn had to go to the very foot of a staircase to rescue Enoch, who now seemed intent on going off permanently at a right angle to the course. The second occasion might have turned out awkwardly for them, for Enoch, in his rudderless stupor, went through the open door of Goronwy Blamey, a broad, jealous, fierce man, who lived under the constant delusion of being betrayed on every front by his wife, Gloria Blamey, who had once been an usherette and nimble in the use of her eyes in 'The Cosy', a cinema of Meadow Prospect where the town seemed to garage the central part of its libido. That afternoon, Goronwy, who had been celebrating the morning of the bank holiday with a few pints in the Con Club, had been letting it in for Gloria on a piled up series of charges and cuffing her in and out of the kitchen, working to a familiar pattern of violence that allowed them both to grab something to eat from the shelves as he backed her into the larder at regular points of climax, Goronwy carrying on just like Othello but smaller, less able at speech, and nowhere near as subtle. But Gloria had given him a fish and chip dinner, which always agreed with Goronwy when on the beer, and his mood had softened to a frenzy of wanting, and they had gone upstairs to an eager rhythm. It was when Goronwy was coming out of the kitchen, his mouth smiling and his braces dangling, with a cup of tea to take up to Gloria, who had just made him promise to be less of a silly billy in the future and to put aside his tormenting visions of men coming in and out of the house, love bent, that he saw Enoch and Onllwyn, apparently naked except for a few strips of cotton, come through the front door at a tremendous pace, heading straight for the stairs as if this had long been their rallying point.

"So these are the games that go on behind my back!" shouted Goronwy; "The rodneys are not even properly dressed." And he waded into Enoch with all his strength, boxing him hard about the head, sparing one for Onllwyn whenever the latter stuck his head in the way. But he did not single out Onllwyn, for he was reserving him as an item that could be properly dealt with when Vizard was dead. It was Verdun who put an end to this by tugging at Goronwy's sleeve and saying: There's a fire upstairs, mate. A look that had wings of longing and terror came to Goronwy's face and he vanished aloft.

They got Enoch on the road again. But his experience with Blamey had finished off all his sense of balance and he was walking now with a kind of extreme left-ward crouch that had the most baffling effect on Onllwyn. They came to a sharp slope on the left. Enoch went down it like a plummet and entered neatly into a bus that chanced to stop at the precise moment of Enoch's arrival at the foot of the slope. The conductor of the bus tried not to look surprised and rang the bell to proceed. Onllwyn wanted to follow him and get him back, but the boys dissuaded him.

"But what'll he do?" asked Onllwyn. "He's got no kind of bus-fare on him in that costume, and in the state he's in he won't be able to explain even by signs what he's doing dressed in that fashion on a bus to Cwmycysgod or some such place."

"Don't worry," said Verdun. "The conductor of that bus is Morlais Morgan, my cousin, who takes a broad view of the bus company and is full of sympathy for all such elements as Enoch who don't know where they're going or what they are up to. Think of yourself now, Uncle Onllwyn. The race is to the swift. You've been waiting years for the chance to show people what you're made of. This is your day, Uncle Onllwyn. You are crying out to Gito that the years of waiting are at an end. Let liars and madmen like Moore and Vizard find their own way to the culvert. Why should sorrow and pity be pulling you down for ever into the marsh? Here we are at the homestretch, the new bypass to the 'Ark'. Hargreaves is waiting there with the money which will buy you those tools and the smallholding with its promise of new life for you and perhaps for us, too, if you can branch out with the right kind of crops and cattle."

Onllwyn's face brightened as if a load had been taken off his spirit.

"You're right, boy. I owe it to Gito, to whom I must be a kind of son. I owe it to him and to me to shout up to life to waggle it about a bit and stop letting me have the whole torrent."

There was only one other competitor in sight as Onllwyn started on his last magnificent spurt along the new road, and as there was no second prize he gave up the ghost as he saw the quality of Onllwyn's final effort. As he breasted the tape there was no cheering from the compact, excited group that had formed around the door of the 'Ark'. Verdun noticed that Cynlais Moore was in the centre of this group, and there was a flushed, depleted look on his face, as if he had just finished a long speech.

"I was first," said Onllwyn humbly.

"First!" said Hargreaves. "You, first! And no wonder. I have been a fancier in every kind of sport you can mention, but I've never come up against a dirtier passage of work than we've seen here this afternoon. And never do I wish to set eyes on another such scoundrel as you, Evans."

Onllwyn did not protest. He simply dropped on to one knee, resting the knee-cap on one of the meagre bits of turf still left outside the 'Ark'.

"Go on," he said, as interested as if Hargreaves were putting on a drama.

"Moore has told us everything. The rupture-stunt with the leg-twists, I saw that myself and it's definitely booked for *The News of the World*. I saw the poor chap curved like an S with you bending over him trying to tie a fourth knot in his legs and cajoling Moore, who was stupefied with pain, to pull it a little tighter. It was cruel. Moore also tells me you had his drawers specially shrunk and if he had raced with those articles pulling at him his manhood would not have survived the first yard. Then there was that caper with the coffin. Who ever heard of anybody but a pagan stretching himself out in dung to get supple? No wonder things have go so lack in Meadow Prospect with boys like you badgering the Christians, Evans. But the final crime was those grips. The last time I saw contraptions of that kind was with a horse dentist, and he was keen on big horses. A deliberate attempt to choke Moore. I've talked it over with the boys here and they agree that short of handing you over to the police the best thing to do is give the prize money to Moore."

"All right," said Onllwyn. "Give it to Cynlais. Cynlais has many needs."

Cynlais was delighted. He rushed into the 'Ark'. When he came out, dressed, he was holding up the prize money.

"Free beer for you boys tonight," he said. "This night will belong to Cynlais Moore."

"Don't forget Elvira's tonics," said Onllwyn.

"She's having Teifion Farr in now for massage. He's a marvel."

"Don't forget Maldwyn's bare behind. He can't sing as he is."

"To hell with Maldwyn. His butts are better bare, and in any case I've trained him to sing with his front to the public."

"If you'll let me," said Elwyn quietly to Onllwyn, "I'll take Cynlais around the back and bring you a part of his head as consolation prize. What bit of Cynlais do you most fancy?"

"Oh never mind, Elwyn. Nice of you to offer, but Cynlais is all right. Slow to learn, that's all."

Onllwyn slipped in for his clothes. The boys remained outside, thinking of Cynlais and of learning and pondering the notion of slowness. As they were about to set out, with Onllwyn between them, Verdun slipped back to the group which was still standing around the front door of the 'Ark', laughing and congratulating Cynlais.

"I wasn't going to tell you this," said Verdun. "But just in case I forget and people start wondering, Uncle Onllwyn also did away with Enoch Vizard half-way through the race. He's really ruthless, is Onllwyn."

He turned a satisfied back on the gaping silence that fell upon the group. He ran to join his friends and they made their way to the Library and Institute, where, that evening, the librarian, Salathiel Cull, known as Cull the Lull, because he was a political quietist and a proponent of gradualist views, was going to give them a talk on why the world's great herds of driven folk should huddle into a compact and cosy mass and let evil bite them to the heart until its teeth were worn to the unhurting stump.

Postscript

'The Face Of Our Jokes' and 'Sitting The Monsoon Out' appeared in *King* in 1964; 'The Putters-Out' was a BBC Morning Story in 1958 and again in 1964, and appeared in *Cover* Magazine in 1972; 'The Heist' was broadcast on BBC Radio Wales in 1972 and was published under the title 'Trigger' in a glossy magazine which I have been unable to identify; 'The Welsh Dreamer' appeared in the *Liverpool Post* in 1977; 'The Little Baron' appeared in *Vogue* in 1958; 'Cover My Flank' appeared in *Cover* in 1971; 'As On A Darkling Plain' appeared in *Masses and Mainstream* in 1948; 'Thy Need' was in *Welsh Short Stories* edited by Gwyn Jones for OUP in 1955; 'No Dancing On The Nerve-Ends, Please' is here published as far as we know for the first time; and all the rest of the stories appeared in *Punch* between 1953 and 1968.

Only a little of Gwyn Thomas's writing is currently in print. Here is a brief list of what is available:

A Welsh Eye, in a large-format paperback, illustrated with sketches by John Dd Evans, published by Hutchinson in 1984; no longer in print but can be found in several South Wales bookshops.

All Things Betray Thee, in a paperback edition with an Introduction by Raymond Williams, published by Lawrence and Wishart in 1986.

Sorrow For Thy Sons, Gwyn Thomas's first novel, written in 1936 but lost until published in paperback with an Introduction by Dai Smith; from Lawrence and Wishart in 1986.

A Few Selected Exits, his autobiography, first published in 1968, reissued in paperback by Seren Books (Poetry Wales Press) in 1985.

Selected Short Stories, seventeen stories chosen from Gwyn Thomas's published short story collections, published by Poetry Wales Press in 1984 in both hardback and paperback; the edition sold out and a new, expanded edition containing six extra stories and an introductory essay by Michael Parnell, appeared in October 1988; it contains among other things 'The Pot of Gold At Fear's End', 'The Leaf That Burns The Hand' and 'Arrayed Like One Of These'.

The Alone To The Alone, with The Dark Philosophers, a reprint of Gwyn Thomas's classic short novels from the 1940's, together in one volume, was published by Golden Grove Press in November 1988.

The Thinker And The Thrush, a very funny novel written in 1947 but never published because of copyright problems between publishers, was published at last by Lawrence and Wishart in November 1988.

Gwyn Thomas:Three Plays, edited by Michael Parnell, was published by Seren Books in October 1990 for the University of Wales Association for the Study of Welsh Writing in English. The volume includes *The Keep, Jackie the Jumper* and *Loud Organs.*